50 Kid Dinner Recipes for Home

By: Kelly Johnson

Table of Contents

- Mini Taco Cups
- Chicken Quesadillas
- Macaroni and Cheese
- Baked Chicken Tenders
- Sloppy Joes
- Pizza Bagels
- Mini Meatloaves
- Chicken Alfredo Pasta
- Homemade Fish Sticks
- Stuffed Bell Peppers
- Vegetable Stir-Fry with Rice
- Spaghetti and Meatballs
- Cheesy Nachos
- Sweet and Sour Chicken
- Sloppy Joe Stuffed Potatoes
- Chicken and Cheese Empanadas
- Mini Pita Pizzas
- Vegetable Fried Rice
- Baked Ziti
- Taco Salad
- Chicken Parmesan
- Homemade Chicken Nuggets
- Cheesy Broccoli Rice Casserole
- Breakfast-for-Dinner Pancakes
- Turkey and Cheese Roll-Ups
- Mini Cheeseburgers
- Stuffed Pasta Shells
- Beef and Cheese Taquitos
- Chicken Tacos
- Simple Chili
- Veggie-Packed Meatballs
- Mac and Cheese Muffins

- Easy Chicken Pot Pie
- Homemade Pizza Rolls
- Sweet Potato Fries
- Turkey Sloppy Joes
- Pasta with Tomato Sauce
- Chicken and Veggie Skewers
- Cheesy Cornbread
- Teriyaki Chicken Bowls
- Mini Quiches
- Pasta Primavera
- Taco-Stuffed Avocados
- Chicken and Rice Casserole
- Vegetable Soup
- BBQ Chicken Wraps
- Cheese and Veggie Stuffed Mushrooms
- Turkey Meatball Subs
- Chicken Burrito Bowls
- Pita Bread Pizzas

Mini Taco Cups

Ingredients:

- 1 pound ground beef (or turkey)
- 1 packet taco seasoning
- 1 cup shredded cheddar cheese
- 1 cup salsa
- 12 small flour or corn tortillas
- Optional toppings: shredded lettuce, diced tomatoes, sour cream, sliced olives, chopped cilantro

Instructions:

1. **Preheat Oven:** Preheat your oven to 375°F (190°C).
2. **Cook Meat:** In a skillet over medium heat, cook the ground beef until fully browned. Drain any excess fat. Stir in the taco seasoning and mix well.
3. **Prepare Tortillas:** Using a round cookie cutter or the rim of a glass, cut out small circles from the tortillas. You'll need enough to fit into a mini muffin tin.
4. **Assemble Cups:** Lightly spray the mini muffin tin with cooking spray. Press each tortilla circle into the muffin cups to form little cups.
5. **Add Meat:** Spoon the cooked taco meat into each tortilla cup.
6. **Add Cheese:** Sprinkle shredded cheddar cheese on top of the meat in each cup.
7. **Bake:** Bake in the preheated oven for about 10 minutes, or until the cheese is melted and the tortillas are crispy.
8. **Top and Serve:** Let the mini taco cups cool slightly. Top with salsa and any optional toppings you like.
9. **Enjoy:** Serve warm and enjoy!

Feel free to customize the toppings to suit your kids' preferences.

Chicken Quesadillas

Ingredients:

- 1 pound ground beef (or turkey)
- 1 packet taco seasoning
- 1 cup shredded cheddar cheese
- 1 cup salsa
- 12 small flour or corn tortillas
- Optional toppings: shredded lettuce, diced tomatoes, sour cream, sliced olives, chopped cilantro

Instructions:

1. **Preheat Oven:** Preheat your oven to 375°F (190°C).
2. **Cook Meat:** In a skillet over medium heat, cook the ground beef until fully browned. Drain any excess fat. Stir in the taco seasoning and mix well.
3. **Prepare Tortillas:** Using a round cookie cutter or the rim of a glass, cut out small circles from the tortillas. You'll need enough to fit into a mini muffin tin.
4. **Assemble Cups:** Lightly spray the mini muffin tin with cooking spray. Press each tortilla circle into the muffin cups to form little cups.
5. **Add Meat:** Spoon the cooked taco meat into each tortilla cup.
6. **Add Cheese:** Sprinkle shredded cheddar cheese on top of the meat in each cup.
7. **Bake:** Bake in the preheated oven for about 10 minutes, or until the cheese is melted and the tortillas are crispy.
8. **Top and Serve:** Let the mini taco cups cool slightly. Top with salsa and any optional toppings you like.
9. **Enjoy:** Serve warm and enjoy!

Feel free to customize the toppings to suit your kids' preferences.

Macaroni and Cheese

Ingredients:

- 2 cups elbow macaroni
- 2 cups shredded sharp cheddar cheese
- 1/2 cup grated Parmesan cheese
- 2 cups milk
- 1/4 cup butter
- 1/4 cup all-purpose flour
- 1/2 teaspoon salt
- 1/4 teaspoon black pepper
- 1/4 teaspoon paprika (optional)
- 1/4 teaspoon garlic powder (optional)
- 1/4 cup breadcrumbs (optional, for topping)

Instructions:

1. **Cook Macaroni:** Cook the elbow macaroni according to the package instructions until al dente. Drain and set aside.
2. **Make Cheese Sauce:**
   - In a medium saucepan, melt the butter over medium heat.
   - Stir in the flour and cook for about 1 minute, creating a roux.
   - Gradually whisk in the milk, ensuring there are no lumps. Continue to cook and stir until the mixture starts to thicken.
   - Reduce heat to low and add the shredded cheddar cheese and grated Parmesan cheese. Stir until the cheese is completely melted and the sauce is smooth.
   - Season with salt, black pepper, paprika, and garlic powder if using.
3. **Combine Pasta and Sauce:**
   - Add the cooked macaroni to the cheese sauce, stirring to coat the pasta evenly.
4. **Optional Baking:**
   - For a baked version, preheat your oven to 350°F (175°C).
   - Transfer the macaroni and cheese to a greased baking dish.
   - Sprinkle the breadcrumbs over the top.
   - Bake for 20-25 minutes, or until the top is golden and crispy.
5. **Serve:** Serve hot and enjoy!

This mac and cheese is creamy and delicious straight from the stove, but adding the optional breadcrumb topping and baking it makes it even more delightful.

Baked Chicken Tenders

Ingredients:

- 1 pound chicken tenders
- 1 cup all-purpose flour
- 2 large eggs
- 1 cup breadcrumbs (panko or regular)
- 1/2 cup grated Parmesan cheese (optional)
- 1 teaspoon paprika
- 1/2 teaspoon garlic powder
- 1/2 teaspoon onion powder
- 1/2 teaspoon salt
- 1/4 teaspoon black pepper
- Cooking spray or olive oil

Instructions:

1. **Preheat Oven:** Preheat your oven to 400°F (200°C). Line a baking sheet with parchment paper or lightly grease it with cooking spray.
2. **Prepare Breading Stations:**
    - In one shallow bowl, place the flour.
    - In a second shallow bowl, beat the eggs.
    - In a third shallow bowl, combine the breadcrumbs, Parmesan cheese (if using), paprika, garlic powder, onion powder, salt, and pepper.
3. **Bread the Chicken Tenders:**
    - Dredge each chicken tender in flour, shaking off any excess.
    - Dip it into the beaten eggs, allowing any excess to drip off.
    - Coat it with the breadcrumb mixture, pressing gently to adhere.
4. **Arrange on Baking Sheet:** Place the breaded chicken tenders on the prepared baking sheet. Lightly spray or drizzle the tops with cooking spray or olive oil to help them crisp up.
5. **Bake:** Bake in the preheated oven for 15-20 minutes, or until the chicken is cooked through and the coating is golden brown and crispy. The internal temperature of the chicken should reach 165°F (74°C).
6. **Serve:** Let the chicken tenders cool slightly before serving. They're great with your favorite dipping sauces!

These baked chicken tenders are a healthier alternative to fried versions and are sure to be a hit with kids and adults alike!

Sloppy Joes

Ingredients:

- 1 pound ground beef (or ground turkey)
- 1 small onion, finely chopped
- 1 bell pepper, finely chopped
- 2 cloves garlic, minced
- 1 cup ketchup
- 1/4 cup tomato paste
- 1/4 cup brown sugar
- 1 tablespoon Worcestershire sauce
- 1 tablespoon apple cider vinegar
- 1 teaspoon mustard (yellow or Dijon)
- 1/2 teaspoon paprika
- 1/4 teaspoon black pepper
- 1/4 teaspoon salt
- 4 hamburger buns
- Optional toppings: shredded cheese, pickles, sliced onions

Instructions:

1. **Cook Meat:** In a large skillet over medium heat, cook the ground beef, breaking it up with a spoon, until browned and cooked through. Drain any excess fat.
2. **Add Vegetables:** Add the chopped onion, bell pepper, and garlic to the skillet. Cook until the vegetables are softened, about 5 minutes.
3. **Make Sauce:** Stir in the ketchup, tomato paste, brown sugar, Worcestershire sauce, apple cider vinegar, mustard, paprika, black pepper, and salt. Mix well to combine.
4. **Simmer:** Reduce the heat to low and let the mixture simmer for about 10 minutes, stirring occasionally, until the sauce is thickened and heated through.
5. **Prepare Buns:** While the mixture simmers, toast the hamburger buns if desired.
6. **Serve:** Spoon the Sloppy Joe mixture onto the bottom half of each bun. Top with any optional toppings you like, then place the top half of the bun on top.
7. **Enjoy:** Serve hot and enjoy!

These Sloppy Joes are easy to make and perfect for a family meal. They're also great for leftovers!

Pizza Bagels

Ingredients:

- 4 plain bagels (split in half)
- 1/2 cup pizza sauce (store-bought or homemade)
- 1 cup shredded mozzarella cheese
- 1/4 cup grated Parmesan cheese (optional)
- 1/2 cup sliced pepperoni or other toppings (like sliced bell peppers, mushrooms, or olives)
- 1/2 teaspoon dried oregano
- 1/4 teaspoon garlic powder (optional)
- Fresh basil or parsley for garnish (optional)

Instructions:

1. **Preheat Oven:** Preheat your oven to 400°F (200°C). Line a baking sheet with parchment paper or aluminum foil.
2. **Prepare Bagels:** Place the bagel halves, cut side up, on the prepared baking sheet.
3. **Add Sauce:** Spread a tablespoon of pizza sauce on each bagel half.
4. **Add Cheese:** Sprinkle shredded mozzarella cheese evenly over the sauce on each bagel. Add grated Parmesan cheese if using.
5. **Add Toppings:** Place your desired toppings (e.g., pepperoni, bell peppers, mushrooms) on top of the cheese.
6. **Season:** Sprinkle a pinch of dried oregano and garlic powder over each bagel for extra flavor.
7. **Bake:** Bake in the preheated oven for about 10-12 minutes, or until the cheese is melted and bubbly, and the bagel edges are lightly browned.
8. **Garnish (Optional):** Remove from the oven and let cool slightly. Garnish with fresh basil or parsley if desired.
9. **Serve:** Serve warm and enjoy!

These Pizza Bagels are super customizable and can be topped with whatever ingredients your kids love. They're a quick and delicious way to enjoy pizza flavors at home!

Mini Meatloaves

Ingredients:

- 1 pound ground beef (or a mix of beef and pork)
- 1/2 cup breadcrumbs
- 1/4 cup grated Parmesan cheese
- 1/4 cup milk
- 1/4 cup ketchup
- 1 large egg
- 1 small onion, finely chopped
- 2 cloves garlic, minced
- 1 teaspoon dried oregano
- 1/2 teaspoon salt
- 1/2 teaspoon black pepper
- 1/2 cup ketchup (for topping)
- Optional: 1 tablespoon brown sugar (to mix with the topping ketchup)

Instructions:

1. **Preheat Oven:** Preheat your oven to 375°F (190°C). Lightly grease a muffin tin or line it with paper liners.
2. **Prepare Meat Mixture:**
    - In a large bowl, combine the ground beef, breadcrumbs, Parmesan cheese, milk, ketchup, egg, chopped onion, minced garlic, dried oregano, salt, and black pepper.
    - Mix until well combined, but don't overmix to keep the meatloaves tender.
3. **Form Mini Meatloaves:**
    - Divide the meat mixture evenly and shape into 12 small meatloaves, placing each one into a muffin cup.
4. **Add Topping:**
    - In a small bowl, mix the 1/2 cup of ketchup with brown sugar (if using). Spoon a small amount of this mixture on top of each mini meatloaf.
5. **Bake:**
    - Bake in the preheated oven for 20-25 minutes, or until the internal temperature of the meatloaves reaches 160°F (71°C) and they are cooked through.
6. **Cool and Serve:**
    - Let the mini meatloaves cool slightly before removing them from the muffin tin.
    - Serve warm.

These Mini Meatloaves are a great way to serve a classic dish in a fun, individual portion. They're perfect for little hands and can be paired with a variety of sides for a complete meal.

Chicken Alfredo Pasta

Ingredients:

- 2 boneless, skinless chicken breasts
- 8 ounces fettuccine pasta
- 2 tablespoons olive oil
- Salt and black pepper, to taste
- 1/2 teaspoon garlic powder
- 1/2 teaspoon dried Italian seasoning (optional)
- 3 cloves garlic, minced
- 1 cup heavy cream
- 1 cup grated Parmesan cheese
- 1/4 cup chopped fresh parsley (optional, for garnish)
- 1/2 cup frozen peas (optional, for added veggies)

Instructions:

1. **Cook Pasta:**
   - Cook the fettuccine according to the package instructions until al dente. Drain and set aside.
2. **Prepare Chicken:**
   - Season the chicken breasts with salt, black pepper, garlic powder, and Italian seasoning (if using).
   - Heat olive oil in a large skillet over medium heat. Add the chicken breasts and cook for about 6-7 minutes per side, or until the chicken is fully cooked and reaches an internal temperature of 165°F (74°C). Remove the chicken from the skillet and let it rest for a few minutes before slicing into strips or cubes.
3. **Make Alfredo Sauce:**
   - In the same skillet, add a little more olive oil if needed and sauté the minced garlic until fragrant, about 1 minute.
   - Reduce heat to low and pour in the heavy cream, stirring to combine with the garlic. Simmer gently for about 2-3 minutes, or until the cream starts to thicken.
   - Gradually whisk in the grated Parmesan cheese until the sauce is smooth and creamy. Season with additional salt and pepper to taste.
4. **Combine Pasta and Chicken:**
   - Add the cooked fettuccine to the Alfredo sauce, tossing to coat the pasta evenly.
   - If using, add the frozen peas and stir until they are heated through.
5. **Serve:**
   - Serve the pasta in bowls, topped with sliced or cubed chicken.
   - Garnish with chopped fresh parsley if desired.
6. **Enjoy:** Serve warm and enjoy your creamy Chicken Alfredo Pasta!

This dish is rich and flavorful, making it a favorite for family dinners. You can also add veggies like broccoli or spinach for extra nutrition.

Homemade Fish Sticks

Ingredients:

- 1 pound firm white fish fillets (such as cod, haddock, or tilapia)
- 1/2 cup all-purpose flour
- 2 large eggs
- 1 cup breadcrumbs (panko or regular)
- 1/2 cup grated Parmesan cheese (optional)
- 1 teaspoon paprika
- 1/2 teaspoon garlic powder
- 1/2 teaspoon onion powder
- 1/2 teaspoon salt
- 1/4 teaspoon black pepper
- Cooking spray or olive oil

Instructions:

1. **Preheat Oven:** Preheat your oven to 425°F (220°C). Line a baking sheet with parchment paper or lightly grease it with cooking spray.
2. **Prepare Fish:**
   - Pat the fish fillets dry with paper towels. Cut them into stick-shaped pieces, about 1/2-inch wide.
3. **Set Up Breading Stations:**
   - In a shallow bowl, place the flour.
   - In a second shallow bowl, beat the eggs.
   - In a third shallow bowl, combine the breadcrumbs, Parmesan cheese (if using), paprika, garlic powder, onion powder, salt, and black pepper.
4. **Bread the Fish Sticks:**
   - Dredge each fish stick in flour, shaking off any excess.
   - Dip it into the beaten eggs, allowing any excess to drip off.
   - Coat it with the breadcrumb mixture, pressing gently to adhere.
5. **Arrange on Baking Sheet:**
   - Place the breaded fish sticks on the prepared baking sheet. Lightly spray or drizzle the tops with cooking spray or olive oil to help them crisp up.
6. **Bake:**
   - Bake in the preheated oven for 12-15 minutes, or until the fish sticks are golden brown and crispy, and the internal temperature of the fish reaches 145°F (63°C).
7. **Serve:**
   - Serve the homemade fish sticks hot with your favorite dipping sauces, such as tartar sauce or ketchup.

Enjoy these crispy and flavorful fish sticks with a side of vegetables or a salad for a complete meal!

Stuffed Bell Peppers

Ingredients:

- 4 large bell peppers (any color)
- 1 pound ground beef (or ground turkey)
- 1 cup cooked rice (white, brown, or a mix)
- 1 can (14.5 ounces) diced tomatoes
- 1/2 cup tomato sauce
- 1 small onion, finely chopped
- 2 cloves garlic, minced
- 1 teaspoon dried oregano
- 1/2 teaspoon dried basil
- 1/2 teaspoon paprika
- 1/2 teaspoon salt
- 1/4 teaspoon black pepper
- 1 cup shredded mozzarella cheese (or cheddar cheese)
- Optional: 1/2 cup corn kernels or cooked black beans for added texture

Instructions:

1. **Preheat Oven:** Preheat your oven to 375°F (190°C).
2. **Prepare Bell Peppers:**
   - Cut the tops off the bell peppers and remove the seeds and membranes. Set aside.
3. **Cook Filling:**
   - In a large skillet, cook the ground beef over medium heat until browned. Drain any excess fat.
   - Add the chopped onion and garlic to the skillet. Cook until the onion is soft and translucent.
   - Stir in the cooked rice, diced tomatoes (with their juices), tomato sauce, oregano, basil, paprika, salt, and black pepper. If using corn or black beans, add them now.
   - Cook the mixture for about 5-7 minutes, stirring occasionally, until everything is well combined and heated through.
4. **Stuff Peppers:**
   - Spoon the meat and rice mixture into each bell pepper, packing it down slightly.
5. **Bake:**
   - Place the stuffed peppers upright in a baking dish. If necessary, trim a small slice off the bottom of each pepper to help them stand up straight.
   - Cover the baking dish with aluminum foil and bake in the preheated oven for 30 minutes.
6. **Add Cheese:**

- Remove the foil, sprinkle the shredded cheese on top of each stuffed pepper, and return to the oven.
- Bake for an additional 10 minutes, or until the cheese is melted and bubbly and the peppers are tender.

7. **Serve:**
    - Allow the peppers to cool slightly before serving. Enjoy!

These Stuffed Bell Peppers are versatile, so feel free to customize the filling with your favorite ingredients or whatever you have on hand.

Vegetable Stir-Fry with Rice

Ingredients:

- 2 cups cooked rice (white, brown, or jasmine)
- 2 tablespoons vegetable oil (or any neutral oil)
- 1 cup broccoli florets
- 1 cup sliced bell peppers (any color)
- 1 cup snap peas or snow peas
- 1 medium carrot, thinly sliced
- 1 cup mushrooms, sliced
- 2 cloves garlic, minced
- 1 tablespoon fresh ginger, minced (optional)
- 1/4 cup soy sauce (or tamari for gluten-free)
- 2 tablespoons hoisin sauce (optional, for extra flavor)
- 1 tablespoon sesame oil (optional, for added flavor)
- 1 tablespoon cornstarch mixed with 2 tablespoons water (optional, for thickening)
- 2 green onions, sliced (for garnish)
- 1 tablespoon sesame seeds (optional, for garnish)

Instructions:

1. **Prepare Rice:**
    - Cook rice according to package instructions. You can use leftover rice for a quicker meal.
2. **Heat Oil:**
    - In a large skillet or wok, heat vegetable oil over medium-high heat.
3. **Cook Vegetables:**
    - Add the broccoli, bell peppers, snap peas, carrot, and mushrooms to the skillet. Stir-fry for about 5-7 minutes, or until vegetables are tender-crisp.
4. **Add Garlic and Ginger:**
    - Add minced garlic and ginger to the skillet and cook for an additional 1-2 minutes, until fragrant.
5. **Add Sauces:**
    - Stir in soy sauce and hoisin sauce (if using). If you prefer a thicker sauce, add the cornstarch mixture and cook for another 1-2 minutes until the sauce thickens.
6. **Add Sesame Oil:**
    - Drizzle sesame oil over the stir-fry for extra flavor, if desired.
7. **Combine with Rice:**
    - Gently fold in the cooked rice, making sure it's well combined with the vegetables and sauce. Heat through for a few minutes.
8. **Garnish and Serve:**
    - Garnish with sliced green onions and sesame seeds, if desired.

9. **Enjoy:**
    - Serve hot and enjoy your delicious Vegetable Stir-Fry with Rice!

This stir-fry is highly customizable, so feel free to add or substitute any vegetables you like or have on hand. You can also add tofu, chicken, or beef for additional protein.

Spaghetti and Meatballs

Ingredients:

For the Meatballs:

- 1 pound ground beef (or a mix of beef and pork)
- 1/2 cup breadcrumbs (plain or Italian)
- 1/4 cup grated Parmesan cheese
- 1/4 cup chopped fresh parsley (or 2 tablespoons dried parsley)
- 1 large egg
- 2 cloves garlic, minced
- 1/2 teaspoon dried oregano
- 1/2 teaspoon dried basil
- 1/2 teaspoon salt
- 1/4 teaspoon black pepper

For the Sauce:

- 2 tablespoons olive oil
- 1 small onion, finely chopped
- 2 cloves garlic, minced
- 1 can (28 ounces) crushed tomatoes
- 1 can (15 ounces) tomato sauce
- 1/4 cup tomato paste
- 1 teaspoon dried oregano
- 1 teaspoon dried basil
- 1/2 teaspoon sugar (optional, to balance acidity)
- Salt and black pepper, to taste

For the Spaghetti:

- 12 ounces spaghetti
- Fresh basil or parsley, chopped (for garnish)
- Grated Parmesan cheese (for serving)

Instructions:

1. **Preheat Oven:** Preheat your oven to 375°F (190°C).
2. **Prepare Meatballs:**
    - In a large bowl, combine the ground beef, breadcrumbs, Parmesan cheese, parsley, egg, minced garlic, oregano, basil, salt, and black pepper. Mix until just combined.
    - Form the mixture into 1 1/2-inch meatballs and place them on a baking sheet.

3. **Bake Meatballs:**
    - Bake in the preheated oven for 20-25 minutes, or until the meatballs are cooked through and have an internal temperature of 160°F (71°C). Set aside.
4. **Prepare Sauce:**
    - In a large skillet or saucepan, heat olive oil over medium heat.
    - Add the chopped onion and cook until softened, about 5 minutes. Add minced garlic and cook for an additional minute.
    - Stir in the crushed tomatoes, tomato sauce, tomato paste, oregano, basil, and sugar (if using). Simmer the sauce for about 15 minutes, stirring occasionally. Season with salt and pepper to taste.
5. **Add Meatballs to Sauce:**
    - Gently add the baked meatballs to the simmering sauce. Let them cook in the sauce for another 10-15 minutes, so they absorb some of the sauce flavors.
6. **Cook Spaghetti:**
    - While the meatballs are cooking in the sauce, cook the spaghetti according to package instructions until al dente. Drain and set aside.
7. **Serve:**
    - Toss the cooked spaghetti with some of the sauce, or serve the sauce and meatballs over the spaghetti.
    - Garnish with fresh basil or parsley and extra grated Parmesan cheese, if desired.
8. **Enjoy:**
    - Serve hot and enjoy your classic Spaghetti and Meatballs!

This recipe is great for a comforting family meal and can be easily doubled for leftovers.

Cheesy Nachos

Ingredients:

- **For the Nachos:**
    - 1 large bag (12-15 ounces) tortilla chips
    - 2 cups shredded cheddar cheese (or a mix of cheddar and Monterey Jack)
    - 1 can (15 ounces) black beans, drained and rinsed
    - 1 cup cooked and seasoned ground beef or shredded chicken (optional)
    - 1 cup sliced black olives (optional)
    - 1 cup diced tomatoes
    - 1/2 cup sliced jalapeños (fresh or pickled, optional)
- **For the Toppings:**
    - 1/2 cup sour cream
    - 1/2 cup salsa
    - 1/4 cup chopped fresh cilantro (optional)
    - 1/4 cup sliced green onions
    - 1 avocado, sliced or mashed (for guacamole, optional)

Instructions:

1. **Preheat Oven:** Preheat your oven to 375°F (190°C).
2. **Prepare Baking Sheet:**
    - Spread the tortilla chips in an even layer on a large baking sheet or oven-safe dish.
3. **Add Toppings:**
    - Sprinkle the shredded cheese evenly over the chips.
    - Distribute the black beans, cooked ground beef or chicken (if using), black olives (if using), diced tomatoes, and sliced jalapeños (if using) over the cheese.
4. **Bake:**
    - Bake in the preheated oven for about 10-15 minutes, or until the cheese is melted and bubbly, and the edges of the chips are slightly crispy.
5. **Add Fresh Toppings:**
    - Remove from the oven and let cool for a couple of minutes.
    - Top with dollops of sour cream, spoonfuls of salsa, chopped cilantro, sliced green onions, and avocado slices or guacamole.
6. **Serve:**
    - Serve warm and enjoy!

These Cheesy Nachos are highly customizable, so feel free to add or substitute any toppings or ingredients you like. They're perfect for game day, movie nights, or any casual get-together!

Sweet and Sour Chicken

Ingredients:

For the Chicken:

- 1 pound boneless, skinless chicken breasts or thighs, cut into bite-sized pieces
- 1/2 cup all-purpose flour
- 1/2 cup cornstarch
- 1 teaspoon salt
- 1/2 teaspoon black pepper
- 1 large egg, beaten
- 1/2 cup vegetable oil (for frying)

For the Sweet and Sour Sauce:

- 1/2 cup white sugar
- 1/2 cup white vinegar
- 1/4 cup ketchup
- 1/4 cup soy sauce (or tamari for gluten-free)
- 1 tablespoon cornstarch
- 1 tablespoon water

For the Stir-Fry:

- 1 tablespoon vegetable oil
- 1 red bell pepper, chopped
- 1 green bell pepper, chopped
- 1 cup pineapple chunks (fresh or canned)
- 1 small onion, chopped
- 2 cloves garlic, minced
- 1 teaspoon ginger, minced (optional)
- 2 green onions, sliced (for garnish)
- Sesame seeds (optional, for garnish)

Instructions:

1. **Prepare the Chicken:**
    - In a bowl, mix the flour, cornstarch, salt, and pepper.
    - Dip each chicken piece into the beaten egg, then coat with the flour mixture.
    - Heat the vegetable oil in a large skillet or wok over medium-high heat.
    - Fry the chicken pieces in batches until golden brown and cooked through, about 4-5 minutes per batch. Remove with a slotted spoon and drain on paper towels.
2. **Make the Sweet and Sour Sauce:**

      - In a saucepan, combine the sugar, vinegar, ketchup, and soy sauce. Bring to a simmer over medium heat.
      - In a small bowl, mix the cornstarch with water to make a slurry. Add this to the simmering sauce, stirring constantly until the sauce thickens (about 2-3 minutes). Remove from heat.
3. **Stir-Fry Vegetables:**
      - In a separate large skillet or wok, heat 1 tablespoon of vegetable oil over medium-high heat.
      - Add the chopped bell peppers, pineapple chunks, and onion. Stir-fry for about 3-4 minutes until the vegetables are tender-crisp.
      - Add the minced garlic and ginger (if using) and stir-fry for an additional minute.
4. **Combine Everything:**
      - Add the cooked chicken pieces to the skillet with the vegetables.
      - Pour the sweet and sour sauce over the chicken and vegetables. Stir to coat everything evenly and heat through.
5. **Serve:**
      - Garnish with sliced green onions and sesame seeds if desired.
      - Serve over cooked rice or noodles.

Enjoy your homemade Sweet and Sour Chicken, which offers a delicious balance of tangy and sweet flavors with crispy chicken and vibrant vegetables!

Get smarter responses, upload files and images, and more.

Sloppy Joe Stuffed Potatoes

Ingredients:

- 4 large russet potatoes
- 1 pound ground beef (or ground turkey)
- 1 small onion, finely chopped
- 2 cloves garlic, minced
- 1 cup ketchup
- 1/4 cup tomato paste
- 1/4 cup brown sugar
- 1 tablespoon Worcestershire sauce
- 1 tablespoon apple cider vinegar
- 1 teaspoon mustard (yellow or Dijon)
- 1/2 teaspoon paprika
- 1/2 teaspoon garlic powder
- 1/2 teaspoon onion powder
- 1/2 teaspoon salt
- 1/4 teaspoon black pepper
- 1 cup shredded cheddar cheese
- 2 tablespoons chopped fresh parsley (optional, for garnish)
- Optional toppings: sour cream, sliced green onions

Instructions:

1. **Bake Potatoes:**
    - Preheat your oven to 400°F (200°C).
    - Pierce the potatoes several times with a fork. Place them on a baking sheet and bake for about 45-60 minutes, or until tender when pierced with a fork.
2. **Prepare Sloppy Joe Filling:**
    - While the potatoes are baking, heat a large skillet over medium heat. Add the ground beef and cook until browned, breaking it up with a spoon. Drain any excess fat.
    - Add the chopped onion and garlic to the skillet. Cook until the onion is softened, about 5 minutes.
    - Stir in the ketchup, tomato paste, brown sugar, Worcestershire sauce, apple cider vinegar, mustard, paprika, garlic powder, onion powder, salt, and black pepper.
    - Simmer the mixture for about 10 minutes, stirring occasionally, until the sauce is thickened and the flavors are well combined.
3. **Stuff the Potatoes:**
    - Once the potatoes are done baking, remove them from the oven and let them cool slightly. Slice each potato in half lengthwise.
    - Use a fork to fluff the inside of each potato and create a small well in the center.

        - Spoon the Sloppy Joe mixture into each potato half, filling it generously.
4. **Add Cheese:**
        - Sprinkle shredded cheddar cheese over the top of each stuffed potato.
5. **Bake Again:**
        - Return the stuffed potatoes to the oven and bake for an additional 5-10 minutes, or until the cheese is melted and bubbly.
6. **Garnish and Serve:**
        - Remove from the oven and let cool slightly. Garnish with chopped parsley, and add optional toppings like sour cream and sliced green onions if desired.
7. **Enjoy:**
        - Serve hot and enjoy your hearty and delicious Sloppy Joe Stuffed Potatoes!

These stuffed potatoes are a great way to enjoy a comforting, classic dish with a fun twist.

Chicken and Cheese Empanadas

Ingredients:

For the Filling:

- 1 pound cooked chicken breast, shredded or finely chopped (use rotisserie chicken for convenience)
- 1 cup shredded cheese (cheddar, Monterey Jack, or a mix)
- 1 small onion, finely chopped
- 1 bell pepper, finely chopped (any color)
- 2 cloves garlic, minced
- 1/2 teaspoon ground cumin
- 1/2 teaspoon paprika
- 1/4 teaspoon chili powder (optional, for a bit of heat)
- Salt and black pepper, to taste
- 1 tablespoon olive oil

For the Dough:

- 2 1/2 cups all-purpose flour
- 1/2 teaspoon salt
- 1/2 cup unsalted butter, cold and cut into small pieces
- 1 large egg
- 1/4 to 1/2 cup cold water (as needed)

For Assembly:

- 1 egg, beaten (for egg wash)
- Optional: 1 tablespoon sesame seeds or poppy seeds (for garnish)

Instructions:

1. **Prepare the Filling:**
    - Heat olive oil in a large skillet over medium heat.
    - Add the chopped onion, bell pepper, and minced garlic. Sauté until the onion is translucent and the bell pepper is softened, about 5 minutes.
    - Stir in the shredded chicken, ground cumin, paprika, chili powder (if using), salt, and black pepper. Cook for an additional 3-4 minutes, stirring occasionally.
    - Remove from heat and mix in the shredded cheese. Let the mixture cool while you prepare the dough.
2. **Prepare the Dough:**
    - In a large bowl, whisk together the flour and salt.

- Cut in the cold butter with a pastry cutter or your fingers until the mixture resembles coarse crumbs.
- In a small bowl, beat the egg and add it to the flour mixture.
- Gradually add cold water, a tablespoon at a time, until the dough comes together and is slightly tacky but not sticky.
- Turn the dough out onto a floured surface and knead gently until smooth. Wrap in plastic wrap and refrigerate for at least 30 minutes.

3. **Assemble the Empanadas:**
    - Preheat your oven to 375°F (190°C) and line a baking sheet with parchment paper.
    - On a lightly floured surface, roll out the dough to about 1/8 inch thick. Use a round cutter (about 4-5 inches in diameter) to cut out circles of dough.
    - Place a spoonful of the chicken and cheese filling in the center of each dough circle.
    - Fold the dough over the filling to create a half-moon shape and press the edges together to seal. You can use a fork to crimp the edges for a decorative touch.
    - Place the filled empanadas on the prepared baking sheet.

4. **Bake:**
    - Brush the tops of the empanadas with the beaten egg for a golden finish. Sprinkle with sesame seeds or poppy seeds if desired.
    - Bake for 20-25 minutes, or until the empanadas are golden brown and crisp.

5. **Serve:**
    - Let the empanadas cool slightly before serving. Enjoy warm or at room temperature.

These Chicken and Cheese Empanadas are great as a meal on their own or paired with a side salad. They also freeze well, making them a perfect make-ahead option!

Mini Pita Pizzas

Ingredients:

- 6 mini pita bread rounds (whole wheat or white)
- 1 cup pizza sauce (store-bought or homemade)
- 1 1/2 cups shredded mozzarella cheese
- 1/2 cup grated Parmesan cheese
- 1/2 cup sliced pepperoni or other preferred toppings (e.g., mushrooms, bell peppers, olives)
- 1/2 teaspoon dried oregano
- 1/2 teaspoon dried basil
- Optional: 1/4 teaspoon red pepper flakes (for a bit of heat)
- Fresh basil or parsley for garnish (optional)

Instructions:

1. **Preheat Oven:**
   - Preheat your oven to 375°F (190°C).
2. **Prepare Pita Bases:**
   - Place the mini pita bread rounds on a baking sheet or pizza stone.
3. **Add Sauce:**
   - Spread a spoonful of pizza sauce evenly over each pita bread, leaving a small border around the edges.
4. **Add Cheese:**
   - Sprinkle shredded mozzarella cheese evenly over the sauce on each pita.
   - Add a sprinkle of grated Parmesan cheese on top of the mozzarella.
5. **Add Toppings:**
   - Add your preferred toppings (e.g., pepperoni slices, mushrooms, bell peppers, olives) on top of the cheese.
   - Sprinkle with dried oregano, dried basil, and red pepper flakes if using.
6. **Bake:**
   - Bake in the preheated oven for 10-12 minutes, or until the cheese is melted and bubbly, and the pita bread is crispy.
7. **Garnish and Serve:**
   - Remove from the oven and let cool slightly.
   - Garnish with fresh basil or parsley if desired.
   - Slice into quarters or serve whole.
8. **Enjoy:**
   - Serve warm and enjoy your Mini Pita Pizzas!

These Mini Pita Pizzas are versatile, so feel free to customize them with your favorite toppings and ingredients. They're great for a quick meal, snacks, or party appetizers!

Vegetable Fried Rice

Ingredients:

- 2 cups cooked rice (preferably cold, as it fries better; day-old rice works great)
- 2 tablespoons vegetable oil
- 1 small onion, finely chopped
- 2 cloves garlic, minced
- 1 cup mixed vegetables (e.g., peas, carrots, corn; fresh or frozen)
- 1 cup bell peppers, diced (any color)
- 1 cup mushrooms, sliced
- 2 large eggs, lightly beaten
- 3 tablespoons soy sauce (or tamari for gluten-free)
- 1 tablespoon oyster sauce (optional, for added flavor)
- 1 teaspoon sesame oil (optional, for extra flavor)
- Salt and black pepper, to taste
- 2 green onions, sliced (for garnish)
- 2 tablespoons chopped fresh cilantro or parsley (optional, for garnish)

Instructions:

1. **Prepare Ingredients:**
   - If you haven't already, cook the rice and let it cool. For best results, use rice that has been cooked and chilled overnight.
   - Chop all vegetables and have them ready to go.
2. **Heat Oil:**
   - Heat vegetable oil in a large skillet or wok over medium-high heat.
3. **Cook Vegetables:**
   - Add the chopped onion to the skillet and cook for about 2 minutes, until it begins to soften.
   - Add the minced garlic and cook for an additional 30 seconds, until fragrant.
   - Stir in the mixed vegetables, bell peppers, and mushrooms. Cook for 4-5 minutes, or until the vegetables are tender but still crisp.
4. **Add Eggs:**
   - Push the vegetables to one side of the skillet. Pour the beaten eggs into the empty side of the skillet and scramble them, cooking until fully set. Once cooked, mix the eggs into the vegetables.
5. **Add Rice:**
   - Add the cold rice to the skillet, breaking up any clumps with a spatula. Stir well to combine with the vegetables and eggs.
6. **Season:**
   - Stir in the soy sauce, oyster sauce (if using), and sesame oil (if using). Mix thoroughly to ensure the rice and vegetables are evenly coated.

- Season with salt and black pepper to taste.
7. **Garnish and Serve:**
    - Garnish with sliced green onions and chopped fresh cilantro or parsley, if desired.
    - Serve hot.

Tips:

- **Rice Texture:** Cold rice works best because it's less sticky and fries up nicely. If using freshly cooked rice, spread it out on a baking sheet and let it cool before using.
- **Veggies:** Feel free to customize the vegetables based on what you have on hand. Other great additions include corn, baby corn, or bean sprouts.
- **Protein:** For added protein, consider adding cooked chicken, shrimp, or tofu to the fried rice.

This Vegetable Fried Rice is a versatile and tasty dish that's perfect for using up leftover rice and veggies. Enjoy it as a side dish or a standalone meal!

Baked Ziti

Ingredients:

- **For the Pasta:**
    - 1 pound (450 grams) ziti pasta (or penne)
    - Salt (for boiling pasta)
- **For the Sauce:**
    - 2 tablespoons olive oil
    - 1 small onion, finely chopped
    - 2 cloves garlic, minced
    - 1 can (28 ounces) crushed tomatoes
    - 1 can (6 ounces) tomato paste
    - 1/2 cup tomato sauce
    - 1 teaspoon dried oregano
    - 1 teaspoon dried basil
    - 1/2 teaspoon sugar (optional, to balance acidity)
    - Salt and black pepper, to taste
- **For the Filling:**
    - 1 1/2 cups ricotta cheese
    - 1 cup grated Parmesan cheese
    - 1 large egg
    - 1 cup shredded mozzarella cheese (plus extra for topping)

Instructions:

1. **Preheat Oven:**
    - Preheat your oven to 375°F (190°C).
2. **Cook Pasta:**
    - Bring a large pot of salted water to a boil. Cook the ziti according to package instructions until al dente. Drain and set aside.
3. **Prepare the Sauce:**
    - While the pasta is cooking, heat olive oil in a large skillet over medium heat.
    - Add the chopped onion and cook until softened, about 5 minutes.
    - Add the minced garlic and cook for an additional 1 minute, until fragrant.
    - Stir in the crushed tomatoes, tomato paste, tomato sauce, oregano, basil, and sugar (if using). Simmer the sauce for 10-15 minutes, stirring occasionally. Season with salt and black pepper to taste.
4. **Prepare the Cheese Mixture:**
    - In a bowl, combine the ricotta cheese, grated Parmesan cheese, and egg. Mix well.
5. **Combine Ingredients:**
    - In a large bowl, toss the cooked ziti with the tomato sauce until well coated.

- Stir in the cheese mixture until evenly distributed.

6. **Assemble the Dish:**
    - Spoon half of the ziti mixture into a large baking dish (about 9x13 inches).
    - Sprinkle half of the shredded mozzarella cheese over the top.
    - Add the remaining ziti mixture on top and finish with the remaining mozzarella cheese.
7. **Bake:**
    - Cover the baking dish with aluminum foil and bake in the preheated oven for 20 minutes.
    - Remove the foil and bake for an additional 10-15 minutes, or until the cheese is melted and bubbly, and the ziti is heated through.
8. **Serve:**
    - Let the baked ziti cool for a few minutes before serving. Garnish with extra Parmesan cheese or fresh basil if desired.

Tips:

- **Make-Ahead:** You can assemble the dish a day in advance, cover it tightly, and refrigerate. Bake it directly from the refrigerator, adding a few extra minutes to the cooking time.
- **Variations:** Add cooked ground beef, sausage, or vegetables (like spinach or mushrooms) to the sauce for added flavor and texture.

Enjoy your comforting and cheesy Baked Ziti!

Taco Salad

Ingredients:

For the Salad:

- 1 pound ground beef (or ground turkey, chicken, or a vegetarian substitute)
- 1 small onion, finely chopped
- 2 cloves garlic, minced
- 1 packet (1 ounce) taco seasoning mix (or homemade seasoning)
- 1/2 cup water (or as directed on seasoning packet)
- 6 cups shredded lettuce (e.g., romaine or iceberg)
- 1 cup cherry tomatoes, halved
- 1 cup diced bell peppers (any color)
- 1 cup black beans, drained and rinsed
- 1 cup corn kernels (fresh, frozen, or canned)
- 1 cup shredded cheddar cheese
- 1/2 cup sliced black olives (optional)
- 1 avocado, diced
- 1/4 cup fresh cilantro, chopped (optional)
- 1/2 cup crushed tortilla chips

For the Dressing:

- 1/2 cup sour cream
- 1/4 cup mayonnaise
- 1 tablespoon lime juice (about 1 lime)
- 1 tablespoon taco seasoning mix (or to taste)
- Salt and black pepper, to taste

Instructions:

1. **Cook the Beef:**
    - In a large skillet, cook the ground beef over medium heat until browned, breaking it up with a spoon. Drain any excess fat.
    - Add the chopped onion and minced garlic to the skillet. Cook until the onion is translucent, about 5 minutes.
    - Stir in the taco seasoning and water. Simmer for about 5 minutes, or until the sauce thickens. Remove from heat and let it cool slightly.
2. **Prepare the Dressing:**
    - In a small bowl, whisk together the sour cream, mayonnaise, lime juice, and taco seasoning mix. Season with salt and black pepper to taste. Set aside.
3. **Assemble the Salad:**

- In a large bowl, combine the shredded lettuce, cherry tomatoes, diced bell peppers, black beans, corn, and shredded cheddar cheese.
- Add the cooked ground beef mixture and toss to combine.
- Gently fold in the diced avocado and chopped cilantro (if using).

4. **Serve:**
    - Just before serving, sprinkle the crushed tortilla chips over the salad for added crunch.
    - Drizzle the taco dressing over the top, or serve it on the side.

5. **Enjoy:**
    - Serve the taco salad immediately and enjoy a fresh, flavorful meal!

Tips:

- **Customizable:** Feel free to add or substitute ingredients based on your preferences, such as sliced jalapeños, chopped green onions, or additional vegetables.
- **Make-Ahead:** You can prepare the salad components in advance but keep the dressing and tortilla chips separate until ready to serve to prevent sogginess.

This Taco Salad is not only delicious but also versatile and can be adapted to suit different dietary preferences. Enjoy!

Chicken Parmesan

Ingredients:

- **For the Chicken:**
    - 4 boneless, skinless chicken breasts (about 6 ounces each)
    - 1 cup all-purpose flour
    - 2 large eggs
    - 1 tablespoon milk
    - 1 1/2 cups Italian-style breadcrumbs
    - 1 cup grated Parmesan cheese
    - 1 cup shredded mozzarella cheese
    - 1 cup marinara sauce (store-bought or homemade)
    - Salt and black pepper, to taste
    - 1/2 teaspoon dried Italian seasoning (optional)
    - 1/4 cup olive oil (for frying)
- **For Garnish:**
    - Fresh basil or parsley, chopped
    - Extra grated Parmesan cheese (optional)

Instructions:

1. **Preheat Oven:**
    - Preheat your oven to 375°F (190°C).
2. **Prepare Chicken:**
    - Place each chicken breast between two sheets of plastic wrap or parchment paper. Use a meat mallet or rolling pin to pound the chicken to an even thickness of about 1/2 inch.
    - Season both sides of the chicken breasts with salt, black pepper, and dried Italian seasoning if using.
3. **Bread the Chicken:**
    - Set up a breading station with three shallow dishes:
        - In the first dish, place the flour.
        - In the second dish, whisk together the eggs and milk.
        - In the third dish, combine the breadcrumbs and grated Parmesan cheese.
    - Dredge each chicken breast in the flour, shaking off excess. Dip in the egg mixture, then coat with the breadcrumb mixture, pressing gently to adhere.
4. **Fry the Chicken:**
    - Heat olive oil in a large skillet over medium-high heat.
    - Add the breaded chicken breasts and cook for 3-4 minutes on each side, or until golden brown and cooked through. The internal temperature of the chicken should reach 165°F (74°C). Transfer the chicken to a paper towel-lined plate to drain.

5. **Assemble the Dish:**
    - Spread a thin layer of marinara sauce in the bottom of a baking dish (about 9x13 inches).
    - Place the fried chicken breasts in the baking dish. Spoon more marinara sauce over each piece of chicken.
    - Sprinkle shredded mozzarella cheese evenly over the sauce.
6. **Bake:**
    - Bake in the preheated oven for 20 minutes, or until the cheese is melted and bubbly, and the chicken is heated through.
7. **Garnish and Serve:**
    - Remove from the oven and let it cool slightly.
    - Garnish with chopped fresh basil or parsley and additional grated Parmesan cheese if desired.
    - Serve with pasta, garlic bread, or a simple salad.

Tips:

- **Homemade Sauce:** For an extra touch, use homemade marinara sauce or your favorite store-bought variety.
- **Freezing:** Chicken Parmesan can be assembled and frozen before baking. Just bake from frozen, adding extra time if needed.
- **Serving Suggestion:** Serve over spaghetti, fettuccine, or with a side of roasted vegetables for a complete meal.

Enjoy your crispy, cheesy, and delicious Chicken Parmesan!

Homemade Chicken Nuggets

Ingredients:

- **For the Nuggets:**
    - 1 pound boneless, skinless chicken breasts or thighs, cut into bite-sized pieces
    - 1 cup all-purpose flour
    - 1 teaspoon salt
    - 1/2 teaspoon black pepper
    - 1 teaspoon paprika
    - 1 teaspoon garlic powder
    - 1 teaspoon onion powder
    - 2 large eggs
    - 1 tablespoon milk
    - 1 1/2 cups breadcrumbs (panko or regular)
    - 1/2 cup grated Parmesan cheese (optional)
    - Vegetable oil (for frying)
- **For Baking (Optional):**
    - Cooking spray or additional oil

Instructions:

1. **Prepare the Chicken:**
    - Cut the chicken into bite-sized pieces. Pat dry with paper towels.
2. **Prepare the Breading Station:**
    - In one shallow bowl, combine the flour, salt, black pepper, paprika, garlic powder, and onion powder.
    - In a second shallow bowl, whisk together the eggs and milk.
    - In a third shallow bowl, mix the breadcrumbs and grated Parmesan cheese (if using).
3. **Bread the Chicken:**
    - Dredge each chicken piece in the seasoned flour, shaking off the excess.
    - Dip in the egg mixture, allowing any excess to drip off.
    - Coat with the breadcrumb mixture, pressing gently to ensure the breadcrumbs adhere well.
4. **Fry the Nuggets:**
    - Heat about 1/4 inch of vegetable oil in a large skillet over medium-high heat.
    - Add the breaded chicken pieces in batches, making sure not to overcrowd the pan. Fry for about 3-4 minutes on each side, or until golden brown and cooked through (the internal temperature should reach 165°F or 74°C).
    - Transfer the cooked nuggets to a plate lined with paper towels to drain excess oil.
5. **Bake the Nuggets (Optional):**

- Preheat your oven to 400°F (200°C).
- Place the breaded chicken pieces on a baking sheet lined with parchment paper or a lightly greased baking rack.
- Lightly spray or brush with oil.
- Bake for 15-20 minutes, flipping halfway through, until the nuggets are golden brown and cooked through.

6. **Serve:**
   - Serve hot with your favorite dipping sauces like ketchup, BBQ sauce, honey mustard, or ranch.

Tips:

- **Make-Ahead:** You can bread the chicken nuggets ahead of time and freeze them. Just place the breaded nuggets in a single layer on a baking sheet and freeze until solid. Transfer to a zip-top bag or airtight container and store in the freezer. Cook from frozen, adding a few extra minutes to the frying or baking time.
- **Healthier Option:** For a healthier version, bake the nuggets instead of frying. They'll still be crispy and delicious.
- **Flavor Variations:** Add different seasonings or spices to the breadcrumb mixture to suit your taste, such as Italian seasoning, cayenne pepper, or dried herbs.

Enjoy your homemade chicken nuggets, which are perfect for a quick meal or a fun snack!

Cheesy Broccoli Rice Casserole

Ingredients:

- **For the Casserole:**
    - 2 cups cooked rice (white or brown)
    - 4 cups fresh broccoli florets (or 1 bag of frozen broccoli, thawed)
    - 2 tablespoons butter
    - 1 small onion, finely chopped
    - 2 cloves garlic, minced
    - 1 can (10.5 ounces) condensed cream of mushroom soup (or cream of chicken soup)
    - 1 cup milk
    - 2 cups shredded cheddar cheese (or a mix of cheddar and Monterey Jack)
    - 1/2 cup grated Parmesan cheese
    - 1/2 teaspoon dried thyme (optional)
    - Salt and black pepper, to taste
- **For the Topping:**
    - 1/2 cup breadcrumbs (panko or regular)
    - 2 tablespoons melted butter
    - 1/4 cup grated Parmesan cheese

Instructions:

1. **Preheat Oven:**
    - Preheat your oven to 350°F (175°C).
2. **Prepare Broccoli:**
    - If using fresh broccoli, steam or blanch it until tender-crisp (about 3-4 minutes). If using frozen broccoli, thaw and drain it.
3. **Cook Onion and Garlic:**
    - In a large skillet, melt 2 tablespoons of butter over medium heat.
    - Add the chopped onion and cook until softened, about 5 minutes.
    - Add the minced garlic and cook for another 1 minute, until fragrant.
4. **Prepare the Sauce:**
    - Stir in the condensed cream of mushroom soup and milk, mixing well until smooth.
    - Add 1 1/2 cups of shredded cheddar cheese and stir until melted and combined.
    - Season with dried thyme (if using), salt, and black pepper to taste.
5. **Combine Ingredients:**
    - In a large bowl, combine the cooked rice, cooked broccoli, and the cheese sauce. Mix well to ensure everything is evenly coated.
6. **Transfer to Baking Dish:**
    - Transfer the mixture to a greased 9x13-inch baking dish.

7. **Prepare Topping:**
   - In a small bowl, mix the breadcrumbs with 2 tablespoons melted butter and 1/4 cup grated Parmesan cheese.
   - Sprinkle the breadcrumb mixture evenly over the top of the casserole.
8. **Bake:**
   - Bake in the preheated oven for 25-30 minutes, or until the casserole is bubbly and the topping is golden brown.
9. **Serve:**
   - Let the casserole cool slightly before serving. Enjoy as a side dish or a main course!

Tips:

- **Rice:** For a creamier texture, use leftover rice or cook the rice slightly underdone, as it will absorb some of the sauce while baking.
- **Vegetable Variations:** You can add other vegetables to the casserole, such as diced carrots, bell peppers, or mushrooms.
- **Cheese:** Feel free to use different cheeses or add a bit of cream cheese for extra creaminess.

This Cheesy Broccoli Rice Casserole is a great way to get veggies into your meal while enjoying a cheesy and satisfying dish. Enjoy!

Breakfast-for-Dinner Pancakes

Ingredients:

- **For the Pancakes:**
    - 1 1/2 cups all-purpose flour
    - 3 1/2 teaspoons baking powder
    - 1 tablespoon sugar
    - 1/2 teaspoon salt
    - 1 1/4 cups milk
    - 1 large egg
    - 3 tablespoons melted butter (plus extra for cooking)
    - 1 teaspoon vanilla extract (optional)
- **For Topping Ideas:**
    - Maple syrup
    - Fresh fruit (e.g., berries, bananas)
    - Whipped cream
    - Chocolate chips
    - Nutella or peanut butter
    - Bacon or sausage (for a savory option)

Instructions:

1. **Prepare the Dry Ingredients:**
    - In a large bowl, whisk together the flour, baking powder, sugar, and salt.
2. **Prepare the Wet Ingredients:**
    - In another bowl, mix the milk, egg, melted butter, and vanilla extract (if using).
3. **Combine Ingredients:**
    - Pour the wet ingredients into the dry ingredients. Stir until just combined. The batter may be slightly lumpy, which is okay. Do not overmix.
4. **Cook the Pancakes:**
    - Heat a large skillet or griddle over medium heat and lightly coat with butter.
    - Pour about 1/4 cup of batter onto the skillet for each pancake.
    - Cook until bubbles form on the surface and the edges look set, about 2-3 minutes. Flip and cook the other side until golden brown, about 1-2 minutes more.
    - Keep pancakes warm in a low oven (about 200°F or 90°C) while you cook the remaining pancakes.
5. **Serve:**
    - Stack the pancakes on a plate and serve with your favorite toppings, such as maple syrup, fresh fruit, whipped cream, or a sprinkle of chocolate chips.

Tips:

- **Customize:** Add mix-ins to the batter, such as blueberries, chocolate chips, or chopped nuts, for extra flavor.
- **Consistency:** If the batter is too thick, add a little more milk, a tablespoon at a time, until you reach the desired consistency.
- **Crispy Edges:** For pancakes with crispier edges, add a little more butter to the skillet between batches.

These pancakes are a versatile and fun option for dinner, offering a sweet and comforting meal that the whole family will enjoy. Enjoy your Breakfast-for-Dinner Pancakes!

Turkey and Cheese Roll-Ups

Ingredients:

- 8 slices deli turkey (thinly sliced)
- 8 slices cheese (such as Swiss, cheddar, or provolone)
- 1/4 cup Dijon mustard or mayonnaise (optional, for spreading)
- 1/4 cup fresh spinach leaves or lettuce (optional)
- 1/4 cup sliced bell peppers or cucumber (optional, for added crunch)
- Salt and black pepper, to taste

Instructions:

1. **Prepare the Ingredients:**
    - Lay out the slices of turkey on a clean surface or cutting board.
    - If using, spread a thin layer of Dijon mustard or mayonnaise on each slice of turkey.
2. **Add Cheese and Vegetables:**
    - Place a slice of cheese on top of each turkey slice.
    - Add a few fresh spinach leaves or a small piece of lettuce on top of the cheese if using.
    - Add a few slices of bell pepper or cucumber for added crunch if desired.
3. **Roll Up:**
    - Starting at one end, carefully roll up each turkey slice tightly around the cheese and any added vegetables.
4. **Serve:**
    - Arrange the roll-ups on a platter. If desired, you can cut them in half to make them easier to handle or serve whole.
5. **Optional Garnish:**
    - Garnish with a sprinkle of salt and black pepper, or serve with toothpicks if you want them to be more appetizer-friendly.

Tips:

- **Variations:** Feel free to experiment with different types of cheese and deli meats. Ham, roast beef, or chicken can be good alternatives to turkey.
- **Add-Ins:** Customize with other add-ins like avocado slices, pickles, or a dash of your favorite seasoning.
- **Make-Ahead:** These roll-ups can be made ahead of time and stored in the refrigerator for up to 2 days. They're great for a quick grab-and-go meal or snack.

Enjoy your Turkey and Cheese Roll-Ups as a simple, satisfying, and nutritious option!

Mini Cheeseburgers

Ingredients:

- **For the Mini Burgers:**
    - 1 pound (450 grams) ground beef (80/20 blend of meat to fat is ideal)
    - Salt and black pepper, to taste
    - 8 small hamburger buns or slider rolls
    - 4 slices cheese (cheddar, American, or your choice), cut into quarters
    - 1 tablespoon vegetable oil or butter (for cooking)
- **For Toppings (Optional):**
    - Lettuce leaves
    - Tomato slices
    - Pickles
    - Ketchup
    - Mustard
    - Mayonnaise
    - Thinly sliced red onion

Instructions:

1. **Prepare the Meat:**
    - In a bowl, gently mix the ground beef with salt and black pepper. Be careful not to overmix, as this can make the burgers tough.
2. **Form the Patties:**
    - Divide the ground beef into 8 equal portions and shape them into small, flat patties. Each patty should be slightly larger than the buns, as they will shrink slightly while cooking.
3. **Cook the Patties:**
    - Heat a large skillet or griddle over medium-high heat. Add a little vegetable oil or butter to the skillet.
    - Cook the patties for about 2-3 minutes on each side, or until they reach your desired level of doneness. For mini cheeseburgers, it's often best to cook them to medium or medium-well.
    - Place a quarter slice of cheese on top of each patty during the last minute of cooking. Cover the skillet with a lid for about 30 seconds to help the cheese melt.
4. **Prepare the Buns:**
    - While the patties are cooking, slice the hamburger buns or slider rolls in half.
    - Optionally, you can toast the buns in a separate pan or under the broiler until they are lightly browned.
5. **Assemble the Mini Cheeseburgers:**
    - Place each cooked patty on the bottom half of a bun.

            - Add your desired toppings, such as lettuce, tomato, pickles, onions, ketchup, mustard, or mayonnaise.
            - Top with the other half of the bun.
    6. **Serve:**
            - Arrange the mini cheeseburgers on a platter and serve immediately while they're hot.

Tips:

- **Cheese Options:** You can use various cheeses like Swiss, provolone, or pepper jack for different flavor profiles.
- **Seasoning:** Feel free to experiment with additional seasonings or mix-ins, like garlic powder, onion powder, or Worcestershire sauce in the ground beef.
- **Make-Ahead:** Cooked mini cheeseburgers can be kept warm in a low oven (about 200°F or 90°C) until ready to serve.

These Mini Cheeseburgers are perfect for parties, family gatherings, or a fun weeknight dinner. Enjoy!

Stuffed Pasta Shells

Ingredients:

- **For the Shells:**
  - 20 large pasta shells
  - Salt (for boiling pasta)
- **For the Filling:**
  - 1 container (15 ounces) ricotta cheese
  - 1 cup shredded mozzarella cheese
  - 1/2 cup grated Parmesan cheese
  - 1 large egg
  - 1 cup fresh spinach, chopped (or 1/2 cup frozen spinach, thawed and drained)
  - 1/2 cup chopped fresh basil or parsley (optional)
  - 1/2 teaspoon dried oregano
  - 1/2 teaspoon dried thyme
  - Salt and black pepper, to taste
- **For the Sauce:**
  - 2 cups marinara sauce (store-bought or homemade)
  - 1/2 cup shredded mozzarella cheese (for topping)

Instructions:

1. **Preheat Oven:**
   - Preheat your oven to 375°F (190°C).
2. **Cook the Shells:**
   - Bring a large pot of salted water to a boil. Cook the pasta shells according to package instructions until al dente. Drain and set aside.
3. **Prepare the Filling:**
   - In a large bowl, combine the ricotta cheese, shredded mozzarella, grated Parmesan, egg, chopped spinach, and fresh basil or parsley (if using). Mix well.
   - Season with dried oregano, thyme, salt, and black pepper to taste.
4. **Prepare the Sauce:**
   - Spread a thin layer of marinara sauce on the bottom of a baking dish (about 9x13 inches).
5. **Stuff the Shells:**
   - Carefully spoon the cheese filling into each cooked pasta shell. Place the filled shells in the baking dish, seam side up.
6. **Add Sauce and Cheese:**
   - Pour the remaining marinara sauce over the stuffed shells. Sprinkle the top with additional shredded mozzarella cheese.
7. **Bake:**

- - Cover the baking dish with aluminum foil and bake in the preheated oven for 20 minutes.
  - Remove the foil and bake for an additional 10 minutes, or until the cheese is melted and bubbly, and the sauce is hot.
8. **Serve:**
    - Let the stuffed shells cool for a few minutes before serving. Garnish with extra fresh basil or parsley if desired.

Tips:

- **Freezing:** Stuffed shells can be assembled ahead of time and frozen. Assemble the dish, cover tightly with plastic wrap and foil, and freeze. Bake from frozen, adding extra time if needed.
- **Variations:** Feel free to add cooked ground beef, sausage, or chopped vegetables (like mushrooms or bell peppers) to the filling for added flavor and texture.
- **Sauce Options:** You can use Alfredo sauce or a combination of marinara and Alfredo for a different twist.

Enjoy your delicious and comforting Stuffed Pasta Shells!

Beef and Cheese Taquitos

Ingredients:

- **For the Filling:**
    - 1 pound ground beef
    - 1 small onion, finely chopped
    - 2 cloves garlic, minced
    - 1 packet (1 ounce) taco seasoning mix
    - 1/2 cup water (or as directed on seasoning packet)
    - 1 cup shredded cheddar cheese (or a mix of cheddar and Monterey Jack)
    - 1/2 cup chopped fresh cilantro (optional)
    - Salt and black pepper, to taste
- **For Assembly:**
    - 12-14 small corn or flour tortillas
    - Vegetable oil (for frying)
- **For Serving (Optional):**
    - Sour cream
    - Salsa
    - Guacamole
    - Shredded lettuce
    - Diced tomatoes

Instructions:

1. **Prepare the Beef Filling:**
    - In a large skillet, cook the ground beef over medium heat until browned, breaking it up with a spoon. Drain any excess fat.
    - Add the chopped onion and minced garlic to the skillet. Cook until the onion is soft and translucent, about 5 minutes.
    - Stir in the taco seasoning mix and water. Simmer for about 5 minutes, or until the mixture is thickened. Season with salt and black pepper to taste.
    - Remove from heat and stir in the shredded cheese and chopped cilantro (if using). The cheese will melt slightly from the heat of the beef.
2. **Prepare the Tortillas:**
    - If using corn tortillas, warm them in a dry skillet or microwave to make them more pliable. This will help prevent them from cracking when rolled.
3. **Assemble the Taquitos:**
    - Place a small amount of the beef and cheese filling in the center of each tortilla.
    - Roll the tortilla tightly around the filling. Secure with a toothpick if necessary to keep the taquito rolled.
4. **Fry the Taquitos:**
    - Heat about 1/4 inch of vegetable oil in a large skillet over medium heat.

- Carefully add the taquitos, a few at a time, to the hot oil. Fry until golden brown and crispy, about 2-3 minutes per side. Use tongs to turn them as needed.
- Transfer the cooked taquitos to a plate lined with paper towels to drain any excess oil.

5. **Serve:**
    - Serve the taquitos hot with your choice of dipping sauces like sour cream, salsa, guacamole, or with a side of shredded lettuce and diced tomatoes.

Tips:

- **Baking Option:** For a healthier option, you can bake the taquitos. Preheat your oven to 400°F (200°C), place the taquitos on a baking sheet lined with parchment paper, and spray lightly with cooking oil. Bake for 15-20 minutes, or until crispy and golden brown.
- **Freezing:** You can freeze assembled, uncooked taquitos. Lay them in a single layer on a baking sheet and freeze until solid, then transfer to a freezer bag. Fry or bake from frozen, adding extra time as needed.
- **Flavor Variations:** Add other ingredients to the filling, such as chopped green chilies, black beans, or diced bell peppers, to customize the flavor.

Enjoy your homemade Beef and Cheese Taquitos!

Chicken Tacos

Ingredients:

- **For the Chicken:**
    - 1 pound boneless, skinless chicken breasts or thighs
    - 1 tablespoon olive oil
    - 1 teaspoon ground cumin
    - 1 teaspoon paprika
    - 1 teaspoon garlic powder
    - 1 teaspoon onion powder
    - 1/2 teaspoon chili powder
    - 1/2 teaspoon dried oregano
    - 1/2 teaspoon salt (or to taste)
    - 1/4 teaspoon black pepper
    - 1/4 teaspoon cayenne pepper (optional, for heat)
    - 1/4 cup chicken broth or water (for extra moisture)
- **For Assembly:**
    - 8 small taco tortillas (corn or flour)
    - Shredded lettuce
    - Diced tomatoes
    - Sliced avocado or guacamole
    - Shredded cheddar cheese or crumbled queso fresco
    - Chopped fresh cilantro
    - Lime wedges
    - Sour cream or Greek yogurt (optional)
    - Salsa or pico de gallo

Instructions:

1. **Prepare the Chicken:**
    - In a small bowl, mix the cumin, paprika, garlic powder, onion powder, chili powder, oregano, salt, black pepper, and cayenne pepper (if using).
    - Rub the spice mixture evenly over the chicken breasts or thighs.
2. **Cook the Chicken:**
    - Heat olive oil in a large skillet over medium heat.
    - Add the chicken and cook for 6-8 minutes on each side, or until the chicken is cooked through and reaches an internal temperature of 165°F (74°C).
    - If needed, add chicken broth or water to the pan to keep the chicken moist and to create a bit of sauce.
    - Remove the chicken from the skillet and let it rest for 5 minutes before slicing or shredding.
3. **Shred or Slice the Chicken:**

- For shredded chicken, use two forks to shred the cooked chicken into bite-sized pieces.
- For sliced chicken, slice the chicken breasts or thighs into thin strips.
4. **Warm the Tortillas:**
    - Heat the tortillas in a dry skillet over medium heat until warm and pliable, or wrap them in a damp paper towel and microwave for about 30 seconds.
5. **Assemble the Tacos:**
    - Place a portion of the cooked chicken in the center of each tortilla.
    - Top with shredded lettuce, diced tomatoes, sliced avocado or guacamole, shredded cheese, and chopped cilantro.
    - Add a squeeze of lime juice and a dollop of sour cream or Greek yogurt if desired.
6. **Serve:**
    - Serve the tacos with salsa or pico de gallo on the side.

Tips:

- **Marinate:** For extra flavor, marinate the chicken in the spice mixture and a bit of lime juice for at least 30 minutes before cooking.
- **Grill Option:** You can also grill the chicken for a smoky flavor. Preheat your grill to medium-high heat and cook the chicken for 6-8 minutes per side, or until fully cooked.
- **Custom Toppings:** Feel free to customize your tacos with additional toppings like pickled onions, jalapeños, or a drizzle of hot sauce.

Enjoy your delicious and customizable Chicken Tacos!

Simple Chili

Ingredients:

- **For the Chili:**
    - 1 pound ground beef (or ground turkey or chicken for a lighter option)
    - 1 medium onion, finely chopped
    - 2 cloves garlic, minced
    - 1 bell pepper (any color), chopped
    - 1 can (15 ounces) diced tomatoes
    - 1 can (15 ounces) kidney beans, drained and rinsed
    - 1 can (15 ounces) black beans, drained and rinsed
    - 1 cup beef broth (or chicken broth for a lighter version)
    - 2 tablespoons tomato paste
    - 1 tablespoon chili powder
    - 1 teaspoon ground cumin
    - 1 teaspoon smoked paprika (optional, for a smoky flavor)
    - 1/2 teaspoon dried oregano
    - Salt and black pepper, to taste
    - 1/4 teaspoon cayenne pepper (optional, for extra heat)
- **For Garnishing (Optional):**
    - Shredded cheddar cheese
    - Sour cream or Greek yogurt
    - Chopped fresh cilantro
    - Sliced green onions
    - Crumbled tortilla chips or crushed crackers

Instructions:

1. **Cook the Meat:**
    - In a large pot or Dutch oven, cook the ground beef over medium heat until browned, breaking it up with a spoon. Drain any excess fat.
2. **Add Vegetables:**
    - Add the chopped onion, garlic, and bell pepper to the pot. Cook until the vegetables are softened, about 5 minutes.
3. **Add Seasonings:**
    - Stir in the chili powder, ground cumin, smoked paprika (if using), dried oregano, salt, black pepper, and cayenne pepper (if using). Cook for 1 minute to toast the spices.
4. **Add Tomatoes and Beans:**
    - Stir in the diced tomatoes, tomato paste, kidney beans, black beans, and beef broth. Mix well to combine.
5. **Simmer the Chili:**

- Bring the chili to a boil, then reduce the heat to low and let it simmer uncovered for 20-30 minutes, or until the flavors are well combined and the chili has thickened. Stir occasionally.
6. **Adjust Seasoning:**
    - Taste the chili and adjust seasoning with additional salt, pepper, or spices if needed.
7. **Serve:**
    - Ladle the chili into bowls and garnish with your choice of toppings, such as shredded cheddar cheese, sour cream, chopped cilantro, sliced green onions, or crumbled tortilla chips.

Tips:

- **Make-Ahead:** Chili often tastes even better the next day as the flavors continue to meld. You can make it ahead of time and store it in the refrigerator for up to 3 days or freeze it for up to 3 months.
- **Vegetarian Version:** For a vegetarian chili, omit the meat and add extra beans or vegetables. You can also use vegetable broth in place of beef broth.
- **Spice Level:** Adjust the spice level to your preference by adding more or less cayenne pepper or chili powder.

This Simple Chili is a versatile and comforting dish that's perfect for a weeknight meal or a cozy gathering. Enjoy!

Veggie-Packed Meatballs

Ingredients:

- **For the Meatballs:**
    - 1 pound ground beef (or ground turkey for a leaner option)
    - 1 small zucchini, grated and squeezed to remove excess moisture
    - 1 small carrot, grated
    - 1 cup finely chopped spinach or kale (fresh or frozen, thawed and squeezed dry)
    - 1/2 cup finely chopped onion
    - 2 cloves garlic, minced
    - 1/2 cup breadcrumbs (plain or Italian)
    - 1/4 cup grated Parmesan cheese
    - 1 large egg
    - 1 tablespoon chopped fresh parsley or basil (optional)
    - 1 teaspoon dried oregano
    - Salt and black pepper, to taste
- **For Cooking:**
    - 1-2 tablespoons olive oil (for baking or frying)
- **For Serving (Optional):**
    - Marinara sauce
    - Pasta
    - Fresh basil or parsley for garnish
    - Grated Parmesan cheese

Instructions:

1. **Preheat Oven (if baking):**
    - Preheat your oven to 375°F (190°C). Line a baking sheet with parchment paper or lightly grease it.
2. **Prepare the Vegetables:**
    - Grate the zucchini and carrot. If using frozen spinach, ensure it's well-drained.
3. **Mix the Meatball Ingredients:**
    - In a large bowl, combine the ground beef, grated zucchini, grated carrot, chopped spinach, chopped onion, minced garlic, breadcrumbs, Parmesan cheese, egg, parsley or basil (if using), dried oregano, salt, and black pepper.
    - Mix until everything is well combined. Be careful not to overmix, as this can make the meatballs tough.
4. **Form the Meatballs:**
    - Using your hands or a cookie scoop, form the mixture into 1 to 1.5-inch meatballs. Place them on the prepared baking sheet.
5. **Cook the Meatballs:**
Baking:

      - Bake in the preheated oven for 20-25 minutes, or until the meatballs are cooked through and reach an internal temperature of 160°F (71°C).
6. **Frying:**
      - Heat olive oil in a large skillet over medium heat. Add the meatballs and cook, turning occasionally, until browned on all sides and cooked through, about 8-10 minutes.
7. **Serve:**
      - Serve the meatballs with marinara sauce over pasta, or as a stand-alone dish with a side of vegetables or a salad. Garnish with fresh basil or parsley and extra Parmesan cheese if desired.

Tips:

- **Vegetable Variations:** You can use other vegetables like bell peppers, mushrooms, or sweet potatoes. Just make sure to finely chop or grate them to blend well with the meat.
- **Make-Ahead:** These meatballs can be made ahead of time and stored in the refrigerator for up to 3 days or frozen for up to 3 months. Reheat in the oven or microwave.
- **Sauce Options:** For a different flavor, try serving with barbecue sauce, teriyaki sauce, or a yogurt-based sauce.

These Veggie-Packed Meatballs are a nutritious and delicious way to enjoy meatballs while incorporating more vegetables into your meal. Enjoy!

Mac and Cheese Muffins

Ingredients:

- **For the Mac and Cheese:**
    - 8 ounces (about 2 cups) elbow macaroni
    - 2 cups shredded sharp cheddar cheese
    - 1 cup shredded mozzarella cheese
    - 1/4 cup grated Parmesan cheese
    - 2 cups milk
    - 2 tablespoons butter
    - 2 tablespoons all-purpose flour
    - 1 large egg
    - 1 teaspoon Dijon mustard (optional)
    - Salt and black pepper, to taste
- **For the Topping (Optional):**
    - 1/2 cup panko breadcrumbs
    - 1 tablespoon melted butter
    - 1/4 cup grated Parmesan cheese

Instructions:

1. **Preheat Oven:**
    - Preheat your oven to 375°F (190°C). Grease a muffin tin or line it with paper liners.
2. **Cook the Pasta:**
    - Cook the macaroni according to the package instructions until al dente. Drain and set aside.
3. **Prepare the Cheese Sauce:**
    - In a medium saucepan, melt 2 tablespoons of butter over medium heat. Stir in the flour and cook for about 1 minute, or until the mixture is smooth and bubbling.
    - Gradually whisk in the milk, making sure there are no lumps. Continue to cook, whisking constantly, until the sauce thickens, about 5 minutes.
    - Remove from heat and stir in the cheddar cheese, mozzarella cheese, and Parmesan cheese until melted and smooth. Season with salt, black pepper, and Dijon mustard (if using).
4. **Combine Pasta and Cheese Sauce:**
    - Stir the cooked macaroni into the cheese sauce until well coated.
5. **Mix in the Egg:**
    - Beat the egg and stir it into the mac and cheese mixture. This helps the muffins hold their shape.
6. **Fill the Muffin Tin:**

- Spoon the mac and cheese mixture into the prepared muffin tin, pressing down slightly to pack it in.
7. **Prepare the Topping (Optional):**
    - In a small bowl, mix the panko breadcrumbs with melted butter and grated Parmesan cheese. Sprinkle this mixture evenly over each muffin.
8. **Bake:**
    - Bake in the preheated oven for 15-20 minutes, or until the tops are golden brown and the muffins are set.
9. **Cool and Serve:**
    - Let the muffins cool in the tin for a few minutes before transferring them to a wire rack to cool completely. Serve warm or at room temperature.

Tips:

- **Add-Ins:** Feel free to mix in extras like cooked bacon bits, diced ham, or vegetables (e.g., peas, chopped broccoli) for added flavor and nutrition.
- **Make-Ahead:** These muffins can be made ahead of time and stored in the refrigerator for up to 3 days. Reheat in the microwave or oven before serving.
- **Freezing:** For longer storage, freeze the cooled muffins in a single layer on a baking sheet, then transfer to a freezer bag. Reheat from frozen in the oven or microwave.

These Mac and Cheese Muffins are a delightful and convenient way to enjoy mac and cheese in a new, portable form. Enjoy!

Easy Chicken Pot Pie

Ingredients:

- **For the Filling:**
    - 2 cups cooked chicken, diced (rotisserie chicken works well)
    - 1 cup frozen peas and carrots (or a mixed vegetable blend)
    - 1 cup frozen corn (optional)
    - 1 small onion, finely chopped
    - 2 cloves garlic, minced
    - 1/4 cup butter
    - 1/4 cup all-purpose flour
    - 1 cup chicken broth
    - 1 cup milk (or half-and-half for a creamier filling)
    - 1 teaspoon dried thyme
    - 1/2 teaspoon dried rosemary (optional)
    - Salt and black pepper, to taste
- **For Assembly:**
    - 1 pre-made pie crust (store-bought or homemade) – or use two if covering top and bottom
    - 1 large egg (for egg wash, optional)

Instructions:

1. **Preheat Oven:**
    - Preheat your oven to 375°F (190°C).
2. **Prepare the Filling:**
    - In a large skillet or saucepan, melt the butter over medium heat.
    - Add the chopped onion and cook until softened, about 3-4 minutes. Stir in the minced garlic and cook for another 1 minute.
    - Sprinkle the flour over the onions and garlic, stirring constantly to form a roux. Cook for 1-2 minutes to remove the raw flour taste.
    - Gradually whisk in the chicken broth and milk. Continue to whisk until the mixture is smooth and begins to thicken, about 3-5 minutes.
    - Stir in the cooked chicken, frozen peas and carrots, frozen corn (if using), dried thyme, dried rosemary (if using), salt, and black pepper. Mix well until the filling is evenly combined. Remove from heat.
3. **Assemble the Pot Pie:**
    - Roll out one pie crust and fit it into a 9-inch pie dish, pressing it into the bottom and sides.
    - Pour the chicken mixture into the prepared pie crust.
    - Roll out the second pie crust and place it over the filling. Trim any excess crust from the edges and crimp the edges together to seal.

- Cut a few small slits in the top crust to allow steam to escape. Brush the top crust with a beaten egg if you'd like a golden finish.

4. **Bake:**
    - Bake in the preheated oven for 30-35 minutes, or until the crust is golden brown and the filling is bubbly.
    - If the edges of the crust start to brown too quickly, cover them with aluminum foil to prevent burning.

5. **Cool and Serve:**
    - Let the pot pie cool for about 10 minutes before serving. This allows the filling to set and makes it easier to slice.

Tips:

- **Make-Ahead:** You can prepare the filling a day in advance and store it in the refrigerator. Assemble and bake the pot pie when you're ready to serve.
- **Frozen Veggies:** Feel free to use fresh vegetables if you prefer. Just make sure they are cooked before adding to the filling.
- **Crust Options:** If you prefer, you can use a store-bought pie crust for both the top and bottom, or make your own pie crust from scratch.

This Easy Chicken Pot Pie is perfect for a comforting dinner and is sure to be a hit with the whole family! Enjoy!

Homemade Pizza Rolls

Ingredients:

- **For the Dough:**
    - 1 1/2 cups warm water (110°F/45°C)
    - 2 1/4 teaspoons active dry yeast (1 packet)
    - 1 tablespoon sugar
    - 3 1/2 cups all-purpose flour
    - 1 teaspoon salt
    - 1/4 cup olive oil
- **For the Filling:**
    - 1 cup shredded mozzarella cheese
    - 1/2 cup grated Parmesan cheese
    - 1/2 cup mini pepperoni or chopped cooked sausage (optional)
    - 1/2 cup pizza sauce (for dipping or spreading)
    - 1 teaspoon dried oregano
    - 1/2 teaspoon dried basil
    - 1/4 teaspoon garlic powder
- **For Baking:**
    - 1 egg, beaten (for egg wash, optional)
    - 1 tablespoon olive oil or melted butter (for brushing)

Instructions:

1. **Prepare the Dough:**
    - In a small bowl, combine the warm water, sugar, and active dry yeast. Let it sit for 5 minutes, or until the mixture becomes frothy.
    - In a large bowl or stand mixer, mix the flour and salt. Make a well in the center and add the yeast mixture and olive oil. Stir to combine.
    - Knead the dough on a floured surface or with a stand mixer fitted with a dough hook for about 5-7 minutes, or until the dough is smooth and elastic.
    - Place the dough in a lightly oiled bowl, cover with a clean towel or plastic wrap, and let it rise in a warm place for about 1 hour, or until doubled in size.
2. **Prepare the Filling:**
    - While the dough is rising, mix the shredded mozzarella, grated Parmesan, and any optional ingredients like pepperoni or sausage. Set aside.
3. **Roll Out the Dough:**
    - Preheat your oven to 375°F (190°C). Line a baking sheet with parchment paper.
    - Punch down the risen dough and transfer it to a lightly floured surface. Roll it out into a rectangle about 1/4 inch thick.
4. **Assemble the Pizza Rolls:**

- Spread a thin layer of pizza sauce over the dough, leaving a small border around the edges.
- Sprinkle the cheese and optional toppings evenly over the sauce.
- Starting from one edge, carefully roll up the dough into a tight log. Pinch the edges to seal.
- Cut the rolled dough into 1-inch pieces and place them on the prepared baking sheet.

5. **Bake:**
   - Brush the tops of the pizza rolls with the beaten egg or melted butter for a golden finish.
   - Bake in the preheated oven for 15-20 minutes, or until the pizza rolls are golden brown and the cheese is melted.

6. **Serve:**
   - Let the pizza rolls cool slightly before serving. Serve warm with additional pizza sauce for dipping.

Tips:

- **Make-Ahead:** You can prepare the rolls in advance and freeze them. After assembling, freeze the rolls on a baking sheet until solid, then transfer to a freezer bag. Bake from frozen, adding a few extra minutes to the baking time.
- **Variation:** Experiment with different fillings such as mushrooms, bell peppers, or olives. You can also use different types of cheese or add a sprinkle of red pepper flakes for extra heat.
- **Dipping Sauces:** Try serving with a variety of dipping sauces, such as marinara, ranch, or garlic butter.

These Homemade Pizza Rolls are a tasty treat that's sure to be a hit with kids and adults alike. Enjoy your homemade, cheesy snacks!

Sweet Potato Fries

Ingredients:

- 2 large sweet potatoes (or 3 medium-sized)
- 2 tablespoons olive oil
- 1 teaspoon paprika
- 1/2 teaspoon garlic powder
- 1/2 teaspoon onion powder
- 1/2 teaspoon ground cumin (optional)
- 1/4 teaspoon cayenne pepper (optional, for heat)
- Salt and black pepper, to taste
- Fresh parsley, chopped (for garnish, optional)

Instructions:

1. **Preheat Oven:**
   - Preheat your oven to 425°F (220°C). Line a baking sheet with parchment paper or a silicone baking mat for easy cleanup.
2. **Prepare the Sweet Potatoes:**
   - Peel the sweet potatoes (optional; you can leave the skin on for extra texture and nutrients).
   - Cut the sweet potatoes into fries or wedges, aiming for uniform size to ensure even cooking. Try to keep the pieces about 1/4 to 1/2 inch thick.
3. **Season the Fries:**
   - In a large bowl, toss the sweet potato pieces with olive oil until evenly coated.
   - In a small bowl, mix the paprika, garlic powder, onion powder, ground cumin, cayenne pepper (if using), salt, and black pepper.
   - Sprinkle the seasoning mixture over the sweet potatoes and toss again to coat evenly.
4. **Arrange on Baking Sheet:**
   - Spread the seasoned sweet potato fries in a single layer on the prepared baking sheet. Make sure there's some space between each fry to ensure they crisp up properly.
5. **Bake:**
   - Bake in the preheated oven for 20-25 minutes, flipping the fries halfway through the cooking time for even crispiness. Bake until the fries are golden brown and crispy on the edges.
6. **Serve:**
   - Remove the fries from the oven and let them cool slightly. Garnish with chopped fresh parsley if desired and serve immediately.

Tips:

- **Crispier Fries:** For extra crispy fries, try soaking the cut sweet potatoes in cold water for 30 minutes before baking. Drain and pat them dry thoroughly before seasoning and baking.
- **Cooking in Batches:** If you have a large quantity, bake the fries in batches to avoid overcrowding the baking sheet. This helps them cook more evenly and become crispier.
- **Dipping Sauces:** Sweet potato fries pair well with a variety of dipping sauces such as ketchup, ranch dressing, honey mustard, or a spicy aioli.

These Sweet Potato Fries are a tasty and healthier alternative to traditional fries and make a perfect side dish or snack. Enjoy!

Turkey Sloppy Joes

Ingredients:

- **For the Turkey Sloppy Joes:**
    - 1 pound ground turkey
    - 1 tablespoon olive oil
    - 1 small onion, finely chopped
    - 1 bell pepper (any color), finely chopped
    - 2 cloves garlic, minced
    - 1 can (8 ounces) tomato sauce
    - 1/4 cup ketchup
    - 2 tablespoons tomato paste
    - 2 tablespoons Worcestershire sauce
    - 1 tablespoon brown sugar
    - 1 teaspoon paprika
    - 1/2 teaspoon ground cumin
    - 1/2 teaspoon dried oregano
    - Salt and black pepper, to taste
    - 1/2 cup water (or chicken broth)
- **For Serving:**
    - 4-6 hamburger buns
    - Optional toppings: sliced pickles, shredded cheese, coleslaw

Instructions:

1. **Cook the Turkey:**
    - Heat the olive oil in a large skillet over medium heat. Add the ground turkey and cook, breaking it up with a spoon, until it is no longer pink and starts to brown, about 5-7 minutes.
2. **Add Vegetables:**
    - Add the chopped onion, bell pepper, and garlic to the skillet. Cook until the vegetables are softened, about 3-4 minutes.
3. **Prepare the Sauce:**
    - Stir in the tomato sauce, ketchup, tomato paste, Worcestershire sauce, and brown sugar. Mix well.
    - Add the paprika, ground cumin, dried oregano, salt, and black pepper. Stir to combine.
4. **Simmer:**
    - Add the water (or chicken broth) to the mixture and stir. Bring to a simmer.
    - Reduce the heat to low and let the mixture simmer uncovered for 10-15 minutes, or until the sauce has thickened and the flavors have melded together. Stir occasionally.

5. **Serve:**
    - Toast the hamburger buns if desired. Spoon the turkey mixture onto the bottom half of each bun.
    - Top with any optional toppings like sliced pickles, shredded cheese, or coleslaw. Place the top half of the bun on the mixture.
6. **Enjoy:**
    - Serve the Turkey Sloppy Joes warm with your favorite side dishes.

Tips:

- **Make Ahead:** You can prepare the turkey mixture ahead of time and store it in the refrigerator for up to 3 days. Reheat before serving.
- **Freezing:** The turkey mixture can be frozen for up to 3 months. Thaw in the refrigerator overnight before reheating.
- **Variations:** Customize your Sloppy Joes with different spices or add-ins like chopped mushrooms, diced carrots, or hot sauce for extra flavor.

These Turkey Sloppy Joes are a great alternative to the traditional version, offering a healthier option without sacrificing taste. Enjoy your meal!

Pasta with Tomato Sauce

Ingredients:

- **For the Pasta:**
    - 12 ounces (about 340 grams) of your favorite pasta (spaghetti, penne, fusilli, etc.)
    - Salt, for the pasta water
- **For the Tomato Sauce:**
    - 2 tablespoons olive oil
    - 1 medium onion, finely chopped
    - 2 cloves garlic, minced
    - 1 can (28 ounces) crushed tomatoes
    - 2 tablespoons tomato paste
    - 1 teaspoon dried basil
    - 1/2 teaspoon dried oregano
    - 1/4 teaspoon red pepper flakes (optional, for heat)
    - Salt and black pepper, to taste
    - 1 teaspoon sugar (optional, to balance acidity)
    - Fresh basil or parsley, chopped (for garnish, optional)
    - Grated Parmesan cheese (for serving, optional)

Instructions:

1. **Cook the Pasta:**
    - Bring a large pot of salted water to a boil. Add the pasta and cook according to the package instructions until al dente.
    - Reserve about 1/2 cup of pasta cooking water, then drain the pasta and set aside.
2. **Prepare the Tomato Sauce:**
    - While the pasta is cooking, heat the olive oil in a large skillet or saucepan over medium heat.
    - Add the chopped onion and cook until softened and translucent, about 5 minutes.
    - Stir in the minced garlic and cook for another 1 minute, being careful not to burn it.
3. **Make the Sauce:**
    - Add the crushed tomatoes and tomato paste to the skillet. Stir to combine.
    - Add the dried basil, dried oregano, red pepper flakes (if using), salt, black pepper, and sugar (if using). Stir well.
    - Bring the sauce to a simmer, then reduce the heat to low. Let it simmer for about 10-15 minutes, stirring occasionally, until the sauce has thickened slightly and the flavors have melded together.
4. **Combine Pasta and Sauce:**

- Add the cooked pasta to the sauce, tossing to coat the pasta evenly. If the sauce is too thick, add a little of the reserved pasta water to reach your desired consistency.
5. **Serve:**
    - Serve the pasta hot, garnished with fresh basil or parsley and grated Parmesan cheese if desired.

Tips:

- **Make it Creamy:** For a creamy tomato sauce, stir in a splash of heavy cream or a couple of tablespoons of cream cheese.
- **Add Protein:** For added protein, top with grilled chicken, meatballs, or sausage.
- **Veggie Additions:** Add vegetables like sautéed mushrooms, bell peppers, or spinach to the sauce for extra nutrition and flavor.

This Pasta with Tomato Sauce is a versatile and comforting dish that's sure to please everyone at the table. Enjoy!

Chicken and Veggie Skewers

Ingredients:

- **For the Skewers:**
    - 1 pound (450 grams) boneless, skinless chicken breasts or thighs, cut into 1-inch cubes
    - 1 red bell pepper, cut into 1-inch pieces
    - 1 green bell pepper, cut into 1-inch pieces
    - 1 medium zucchini, sliced into 1/2-inch rounds
    - 1 small red onion, cut into wedges
    - 8-10 cherry tomatoes
    - 1-2 tablespoons olive oil
    - Salt and black pepper, to taste
- **For the Marinade (Optional):**
    - 1/4 cup olive oil
    - 2 tablespoons soy sauce
    - 2 tablespoons lemon juice or vinegar
    - 2 cloves garlic, minced
    - 1 tablespoon honey or maple syrup
    - 1 teaspoon dried oregano or thyme
    - 1/2 teaspoon smoked paprika or regular paprika
    - Salt and black pepper, to taste

Instructions:

1. **Marinate the Chicken (Optional):**
    - In a bowl, whisk together the olive oil, soy sauce, lemon juice or vinegar, minced garlic, honey or maple syrup, dried oregano or thyme, smoked paprika, salt, and black pepper.
    - Add the chicken cubes to the marinade, toss to coat, and let marinate in the refrigerator for at least 30 minutes or up to 4 hours for more flavor.
2. **Prepare the Vegetables:**
    - Cut the bell peppers, zucchini, red onion, and cherry tomatoes into bite-sized pieces.
3. **Assemble the Skewers:**
    - If using wooden skewers, soak them in water for at least 30 minutes to prevent burning. If using metal skewers, no soaking is necessary.
    - Thread the marinated chicken and vegetables onto the skewers, alternating between the chicken and veggies. Leave a little space between each piece for even cooking.
4. **Cook the Skewers:**
Grilling:

- Preheat the grill to medium-high heat.
- Brush the grill grates with oil to prevent sticking.
- Place the skewers on the grill and cook for 10-15 minutes, turning occasionally, until the chicken is cooked through and has reached an internal temperature of 165°F (74°C) and the vegetables are tender.

5. **Oven Baking:**
    - Preheat the oven to 400°F (200°C). Line a baking sheet with aluminum foil or parchment paper.
    - Place the skewers on the baking sheet and bake for 15-20 minutes, or until the chicken is cooked through and the vegetables are tender. You can also broil the skewers for an additional 2-3 minutes to get a bit of char on the chicken and vegetables.

6. **Serve:**
    - Remove the skewers from the grill or oven and let them rest for a few minutes.
    - Serve warm, garnished with fresh herbs if desired, and enjoy with your favorite side dishes like rice, couscous, or a fresh salad.

Tips:

- **Vegetable Variations:** Feel free to use other vegetables like mushrooms, cherry tomatoes, or corn on the cob. Just ensure they have similar cooking times to the chicken.
- **Marinade Alternatives:** Experiment with different marinades, such as teriyaki, barbecue, or a lemon-herb mix, to suit your taste.
- **Grill Pan:** If you don't have a grill, you can use a grill pan on the stovetop or cook the skewers in the oven under the broiler.

Chicken and Veggie Skewers are a fun and flavorful way to enjoy a healthy meal, and they're perfect for any occasion from casual dinners to barbecue parties. Enjoy!

Cheesy Cornbread

Ingredients:

- **Dry Ingredients:**
    - 1 cup cornmeal
    - 1 cup all-purpose flour
    - 1/4 cup granulated sugar
    - 1 tablespoon baking powder
    - 1/2 teaspoon salt
- **Wet Ingredients:**
    - 1 cup milk
    - 2 large eggs
    - 1/4 cup melted butter or vegetable oil
    - 1 cup shredded cheddar cheese (or your choice of cheese, such as Monterey Jack or a blend)
- **Optional Add-ins:**
    - 1/2 cup chopped jalapeños (for a spicy kick)
    - 1/4 cup chopped fresh chives or green onions (for added flavor)
    - 1/2 cup cooked, crumbled bacon (for extra savory goodness)

Instructions:

1. **Preheat Oven:**
    - Preheat your oven to 400°F (200°C). Grease an 8-inch square baking dish or a similarly sized oven-safe pan, or line it with parchment paper.
2. **Mix Dry Ingredients:**
    - In a large bowl, whisk together the cornmeal, flour, sugar, baking powder, and salt.
3. **Mix Wet Ingredients:**
    - In another bowl, whisk together the milk, eggs, and melted butter or vegetable oil.
4. **Combine Ingredients:**
    - Pour the wet ingredients into the dry ingredients and stir until just combined. Be careful not to overmix.
    - Fold in the shredded cheese and any optional add-ins, if using.
5. **Bake:**
    - Pour the batter into the prepared baking dish and spread it out evenly.
    - Bake in the preheated oven for 20-25 minutes, or until the cornbread is golden brown and a toothpick inserted into the center comes out clean.
6. **Cool and Serve:**
    - Let the cornbread cool in the pan for a few minutes before cutting into squares or slices.
    - Serve warm, optionally with butter or honey.

Tips:

- **Cheese Variations:** Experiment with different types of cheese or a cheese blend for varied flavors.
- **Add-ins:** Customize your cornbread by adding other ingredients like diced bell peppers, onions, or herbs.
- **Storage:** Store leftover cornbread in an airtight container at room temperature for up to 2 days. For longer storage, wrap it tightly and freeze for up to 3 months. Reheat in the oven or microwave before serving.

Cheesy Cornbread is a comforting, flavorful side dish that's sure to be a hit at any meal. Enjoy!

Teriyaki Chicken Bowls

Ingredients:

- **For the Teriyaki Chicken:**
    - 1 pound (450 grams) boneless, skinless chicken thighs or breasts, cut into bite-sized pieces
    - 1 tablespoon olive oil
    - 1/2 cup teriyaki sauce (store-bought or homemade; see recipe below)
    - 1 tablespoon honey or brown sugar (optional, for added sweetness)
    - 1 teaspoon minced garlic
    - 1 teaspoon minced ginger
    - 1 tablespoon cornstarch mixed with 1 tablespoon water (for thickening, optional)
- **For the Bowls:**
    - 2 cups cooked rice (white, brown, or jasmine)
    - 1 cup steamed or sautéed vegetables (e.g., broccoli, bell peppers, snap peas, carrots)
    - 1 tablespoon sesame seeds (for garnish)
    - 2 green onions, sliced (for garnish)
    - Optional toppings: sliced avocado, chopped cilantro, pickled ginger

Instructions:

1. **Cook the Chicken:**
    - Heat the olive oil in a large skillet or pan over medium-high heat.
    - Add the chicken pieces and cook, stirring occasionally, until the chicken is cooked through and browned, about 5-7 minutes.
    - Stir in the minced garlic and ginger, and cook for an additional 1 minute.
    - Pour in the teriyaki sauce and honey or brown sugar (if using). Stir to coat the chicken evenly.
    - If you prefer a thicker sauce, add the cornstarch mixture and cook for another 1-2 minutes until the sauce has thickened.
2. **Prepare the Vegetables:**
    - While the chicken is cooking, prepare your vegetables. You can steam them or sauté them in a separate pan with a little oil until tender-crisp.
3. **Assemble the Bowls:**
    - Divide the cooked rice among serving bowls.
    - Top with the teriyaki chicken.
    - Arrange the steamed or sautéed vegetables around the chicken.
4. **Garnish and Serve:**
    - Sprinkle sesame seeds and sliced green onions over the top.
    - Add any additional optional toppings like sliced avocado, chopped cilantro, or pickled ginger.

- Serve warm and enjoy!

Optional Teriyaki Sauce Recipe:

If you prefer homemade teriyaki sauce, here's a quick recipe:

Ingredients:

- 1/2 cup soy sauce
- 1/4 cup water
- 1/4 cup honey or brown sugar
- 2 tablespoons rice vinegar
- 1 tablespoon cornstarch mixed with 1 tablespoon water (for thickening)
- 1 teaspoon minced garlic
- 1 teaspoon minced ginger

Instructions:

1. Combine all ingredients (except cornstarch mixture) in a small saucepan.
2. Bring to a simmer over medium heat, stirring frequently.
3. Stir in the cornstarch mixture and continue to simmer until the sauce thickens, about 2-3 minutes.
4. Remove from heat and let cool before using.

Tips:

- **Rice Options:** Feel free to use different types of rice or even cauliflower rice for a lower-carb option.
- **Vegetable Variations:** You can use any vegetables you like or have on hand. Just make sure they're cooked to your preferred level of doneness.
- **Make-Ahead:** The chicken and vegetables can be cooked in advance and stored in the refrigerator for up to 3 days. Reheat before serving.

These Teriyaki Chicken Bowls are a tasty and nutritious meal that's easy to prepare and customize to your tastes. Enjoy!

Mini Quiches

Ingredients:

- **For the Crust:**
    - 1 1/2 cups all-purpose flour
    - 1/2 cup cold unsalted butter, cut into small pieces
    - 1/4 cup cold water
    - 1/4 teaspoon salt
- **For the Filling:**
    - 4 large eggs
    - 1 cup milk or heavy cream
    - 1 cup shredded cheese (cheddar, Swiss, or your choice)
    - 1 cup cooked and crumbled bacon, sausage, or diced ham (optional)
    - 1 cup chopped vegetables (e.g., bell peppers, spinach, mushrooms, onions)
    - 1/2 teaspoon dried thyme or oregano
    - Salt and black pepper, to taste

Instructions:

1. **Prepare the Crust:**
    - Preheat your oven to 375°F (190°C). Grease a mini muffin tin or line it with paper liners.
    - In a large bowl, combine the flour and salt. Cut in the cold butter using a pastry cutter or your fingers until the mixture resembles coarse crumbs.
    - Gradually add the cold water, mixing until the dough just comes together. You may need a bit more water if the dough is too dry.
    - Roll out the dough on a lightly floured surface to about 1/8-inch thickness. Cut out circles that are slightly larger than the muffin tin cups (about 2 inches in diameter) and press them into the wells of the tin.
2. **Prepare the Filling:**
    - In a medium bowl, whisk together the eggs and milk or cream. Season with salt and black pepper.
    - Stir in the shredded cheese, cooked meat (if using), chopped vegetables, and dried thyme or oregano.
3. **Assemble and Bake:**
    - Spoon the filling evenly into each prepared crust, filling each cup about 3/4 full.
    - Bake in the preheated oven for 18-22 minutes, or until the quiches are set and lightly golden on top. A toothpick inserted in the center should come out clean.
4. **Cool and Serve:**
    - Let the mini quiches cool in the pan for a few minutes before transferring them to a wire rack to cool completely.
    - Serve warm or at room temperature.

Tips:

- **Make-Ahead:** Mini quiches can be made in advance and stored in the refrigerator for up to 3 days. They can also be frozen for up to 3 months. Reheat in a preheated oven or microwave before serving.
- **Customize Fillings:** Feel free to experiment with different cheeses, meats, and vegetables. Try combinations like spinach and feta, mushroom and Swiss, or bacon and cheddar.
- **Crust-Free Option:** For a lower-carb option, skip the crust and bake the filling in a greased muffin tin for crustless mini quiches.

Mini Quiches are perfect for a variety of occasions, from casual family meals to festive gatherings. Enjoy these versatile and delicious little bites!

Pasta Primavera

Ingredients:

- **For the Pasta:**
    - 12 ounces (340 grams) pasta (penne, fettuccine, or your choice)
    - Salt, for the pasta water
- **For the Vegetables:**
    - 2 tablespoons olive oil
    - 1 small onion, chopped
    - 2 cloves garlic, minced
    - 1 bell pepper (red, yellow, or orange), sliced
    - 1 cup cherry tomatoes, halved
    - 1 cup broccoli florets
    - 1 medium zucchini, sliced
    - 1/2 cup carrots, sliced
    - 1/2 cup peas (fresh or frozen)
    - 1/4 cup grated Parmesan cheese
    - 1/4 cup chopped fresh basil or parsley
    - Salt and black pepper, to taste
    - Optional: 1/4 teaspoon red pepper flakes (for heat)
- **For the Sauce:**
    - 1/4 cup vegetable or chicken broth
    - 1/4 cup heavy cream or milk (optional, for creaminess)
    - 1 tablespoon lemon juice (optional, for brightness)
    - 1 tablespoon olive oil
    - 1 teaspoon dried oregano or Italian seasoning

Instructions:

1. **Cook the Pasta:**
    - Bring a large pot of salted water to a boil. Add the pasta and cook according to the package instructions until al dente. Reserve about 1/2 cup of pasta cooking water before draining.
    - Drain the pasta and set aside.
2. **Prepare the Vegetables:**
    - While the pasta is cooking, heat the olive oil in a large skillet or sauté pan over medium heat.
    - Add the chopped onion and cook until softened, about 3 minutes.
    - Stir in the minced garlic and cook for another 1 minute.
    - Add the bell pepper, broccoli, carrots, and zucchini. Sauté until the vegetables are tender-crisp, about 5-7 minutes.

- Stir in the cherry tomatoes and peas, and cook for another 2-3 minutes until the tomatoes start to soften.
3. **Make the Sauce:**
    - In the same skillet with the vegetables, add the vegetable or chicken broth, heavy cream or milk (if using), and lemon juice (if using).
    - Stir in the dried oregano or Italian seasoning. Let the mixture simmer for 2-3 minutes to combine the flavors.
4. **Combine Pasta and Vegetables:**
    - Add the cooked pasta to the skillet with the vegetables and sauce. Toss to combine, adding a little of the reserved pasta water if needed to loosen the sauce.
    - Stir in the grated Parmesan cheese and chopped basil or parsley. Season with salt, black pepper, and red pepper flakes (if using) to taste.
5. **Serve:**
    - Serve the Pasta Primavera warm, garnished with additional Parmesan cheese and fresh herbs if desired.

Tips:

- **Vegetable Variations:** Feel free to use any seasonal vegetables you have on hand. Mushrooms, asparagus, or snap peas are great additions.
- **Creamy Option:** For a richer dish, you can add a splash of heavy cream or a dollop of ricotta cheese.
- **Protein Additions:** Add cooked chicken, shrimp, or tofu for extra protein.

Pasta Primavera is a colorful and nutritious dish that's easy to adapt to your tastes and the season's best produce. Enjoy this fresh and flavorful meal!

Taco-Stuffed Avocados

Ingredients:

- **For the Taco Filling:**
    - 1 pound (450 grams) ground beef, turkey, or chicken
    - 1 tablespoon olive oil
    - 1 small onion, finely chopped
    - 2 cloves garlic, minced
    - 1 packet (1 ounce) taco seasoning mix (or homemade seasoning, see note)
    - 1/4 cup water
    - 1/2 cup black beans (canned or cooked), drained and rinsed
    - 1/2 cup corn kernels (fresh, frozen, or canned)
- **For the Avocados:**
    - 2 ripe avocados
    - Juice of 1 lime
    - Salt, to taste
- **For Garnish:**
    - 1/2 cup shredded lettuce
    - 1/2 cup diced tomatoes
    - 1/4 cup shredded cheese (cheddar, Monterey Jack, or your choice)
    - 1/4 cup chopped fresh cilantro
    - Sour cream or Greek yogurt (optional, for topping)
    - Salsa or pico de gallo (optional, for topping)

Instructions:

1. **Prepare the Taco Filling:**
    - Heat the olive oil in a large skillet over medium heat.
    - Add the chopped onion and cook until softened, about 3 minutes.
    - Add the minced garlic and cook for an additional minute.
    - Add the ground beef, turkey, or chicken to the skillet. Cook, breaking it up with a spoon, until browned and cooked through.
    - Stir in the taco seasoning mix and water. Mix well and simmer for 3-4 minutes until the sauce thickens slightly.
    - Stir in the black beans and corn. Cook for another 2-3 minutes until heated through. Remove from heat and set aside.
2. **Prepare the Avocados:**
    - Cut the avocados in half lengthwise and remove the pit.
    - Use a spoon to scoop out a little of the flesh from each half to create more room for the filling.
    - Sprinkle the avocado halves with lime juice and a pinch of salt to prevent browning and enhance flavor.

3. **Assemble the Taco-Stuffed Avocados:**
    - Spoon the taco filling into each avocado half, packing it in gently.
    - Top with shredded lettuce, diced tomatoes, and shredded cheese.
4. **Garnish and Serve:**
    - Sprinkle with chopped fresh cilantro.
    - Add a dollop of sour cream or Greek yogurt and/or a spoonful of salsa or pico de gallo, if desired.
    - Serve immediately and enjoy!

Tips:

- **Homemade Taco Seasoning:** If you prefer to make your own taco seasoning, you can mix together 1 teaspoon each of chili powder, cumin, paprika, garlic powder, onion powder, and a pinch of salt and pepper.
- **Vegetarian Option:** Use a plant-based protein or just the beans and corn for a vegetarian version.
- **Avocado Preparation:** If you need to prepare the avocados in advance, be sure to brush them lightly with lemon or lime juice to keep them from browning.

These Taco-Stuffed Avocados are a fun and healthy way to enjoy taco flavors without the usual taco shell. They're perfect for a light meal, appetizer, or even a party platter. Enjoy!

Chicken and Rice Casserole

Ingredients:

- **For the Casserole:**
    - 1 pound (450 grams) boneless, skinless chicken breasts or thighs
    - 1 tablespoon olive oil
    - 1 medium onion, chopped
    - 2 cloves garlic, minced
    - 1 cup long-grain white rice (uncooked)
    - 1 can (10.5 ounces) cream of chicken soup (or cream of mushroom soup)
    - 1 cup chicken broth
    - 1 cup milk
    - 1 cup frozen peas and carrots (or your choice of mixed vegetables)
    - 1 cup shredded cheddar cheese (or your choice of cheese)
    - 1 teaspoon dried thyme
    - 1 teaspoon dried parsley
    - Salt and black pepper, to taste
- **For the Topping (Optional):**
    - 1/2 cup breadcrumbs
    - 2 tablespoons melted butter
    - 1/4 cup grated Parmesan cheese

Instructions:

1. **Preheat Oven:**
    - Preheat your oven to 375°F (190°C).
2. **Cook the Chicken:**
    - Heat the olive oil in a large skillet over medium-high heat.
    - Add the chicken breasts or thighs and cook until no longer pink in the center, about 6-7 minutes per side, depending on thickness.
    - Remove the chicken from the skillet and let it rest for a few minutes. Then, shred or chop the chicken into bite-sized pieces.
3. **Prepare the Casserole Base:**
    - In the same skillet, add the chopped onion and cook until softened, about 3-4 minutes.
    - Stir in the minced garlic and cook for an additional minute.
4. **Combine Ingredients:**
    - In a large mixing bowl, combine the cream of chicken soup, chicken broth, milk, dried thyme, dried parsley, salt, and black pepper.
    - Add the uncooked rice, cooked onion and garlic, shredded chicken, frozen peas and carrots, and shredded cheese. Mix until well combined.
5. **Assemble the Casserole:**

- Transfer the mixture into a greased 9x13-inch baking dish or similar oven-safe dish.
- If using, mix the breadcrumbs with melted butter and Parmesan cheese, and sprinkle evenly over the top of the casserole.

6. **Bake:**
   - Cover the dish with aluminum foil and bake in the preheated oven for 45 minutes.
   - Remove the foil and bake for an additional 10-15 minutes, or until the rice is tender, the cheese is melted, and the topping is golden brown (if using).

7. **Cool and Serve:**
   - Let the casserole cool for a few minutes before serving. This helps it set and makes it easier to serve.

Tips:

- **Vegetable Variations:** Feel free to use other vegetables such as corn, green beans, or bell peppers.
- **Cheese Options:** You can use different types of cheese or add a cheese blend for extra flavor.
- **Make-Ahead:** This casserole can be assembled ahead of time and stored in the refrigerator for up to 2 days before baking. You may need to add a few extra minutes to the baking time if it's cold from the fridge.

Chicken and Rice Casserole is a comforting and versatile dish that's sure to please. Enjoy this easy, flavorful meal with your family!

Vegetable Soup

Ingredients:

- **For the Soup:**
    - 2 tablespoons olive oil
    - 1 medium onion, chopped
    - 2 cloves garlic, minced
    - 2 carrots, sliced
    - 2 celery stalks, sliced
    - 1 bell pepper (red, green, or yellow), chopped
    - 1 zucchini, chopped
    - 1 cup green beans, trimmed and cut into bite-sized pieces
    - 1 cup corn kernels (fresh, frozen, or canned)
    - 1 can (14.5 ounces) diced tomatoes (with juice)
    - 4 cups vegetable broth (or chicken broth)
    - 1 bay leaf
    - 1 teaspoon dried thyme
    - 1 teaspoon dried basil
    - Salt and black pepper, to taste
    - 1 cup spinach or kale, chopped (optional)
    - 1 cup cooked pasta, rice, or quinoa (optional, for added heartiness)
- **For Garnish (Optional):**
    - Fresh parsley, chopped
    - Grated Parmesan cheese
    - Croutons

Instructions:

1. **Sauté the Vegetables:**
    - Heat the olive oil in a large pot or Dutch oven over medium heat.
    - Add the chopped onion and cook until softened, about 3-4 minutes.
    - Stir in the minced garlic and cook for an additional 1 minute.
2. **Add the Vegetables:**
    - Add the carrots, celery, and bell pepper to the pot. Cook for about 5 minutes, stirring occasionally, until they start to soften.
3. **Add Remaining Ingredients:**
    - Stir in the zucchini, green beans, corn, diced tomatoes with their juice, and vegetable broth.
    - Add the bay leaf, dried thyme, dried basil, salt, and black pepper. Stir to combine.
4. **Simmer the Soup:**
    - Bring the soup to a boil. Reduce the heat to low and let it simmer, uncovered, for about 20-25 minutes, or until the vegetables are tender.

5. **Add Optional Ingredients:**
   - If using, stir in the chopped spinach or kale and let it cook for an additional 2-3 minutes until wilted.
   - Add the cooked pasta, rice, or quinoa if desired, and heat through for about 2-3 minutes.
6. **Adjust Seasoning:**
   - Taste the soup and adjust the seasoning with more salt and pepper if needed.
7. **Serve:**
   - Ladle the soup into bowls and garnish with fresh parsley, grated Parmesan cheese, or croutons if desired.

Tips:

- **Vegetable Variations:** Feel free to use any vegetables you have on hand, such as potatoes, butternut squash, or mushrooms.
- **Broth:** For a richer flavor, use homemade vegetable or chicken broth.
- **Spices:** Customize the soup with additional spices or herbs like rosemary, cumin, or paprika to suit your taste.
- **Storage:** Store leftover soup in an airtight container in the refrigerator for up to 4 days or freeze for up to 3 months. Reheat thoroughly before serving.

Vegetable Soup is a versatile and comforting dish that's easy to make and perfect for a healthy meal. Enjoy!

BBQ Chicken Wraps

Ingredients:

- **For the BBQ Chicken:**
    - 1 pound (450 grams) boneless, skinless chicken breasts or thighs
    - 1 tablespoon olive oil
    - 1/2 cup BBQ sauce (store-bought or homemade)
    - 1 tablespoon honey (optional, for extra sweetness)
    - Salt and black pepper, to taste
- **For the Wraps:**
    - 4 large flour tortillas (or your choice of wrap, such as whole wheat or spinach)
    - 1 cup shredded lettuce
    - 1/2 cup sliced red onion
    - 1/2 cup sliced bell peppers (any color)
    - 1/2 cup shredded cheese (cheddar, Monterey Jack, or your choice)
    - 1/4 cup sliced jalapeños (optional, for heat)
    - 1 avocado, sliced (optional)
    - 1/4 cup chopped fresh cilantro (optional)
    - 1/2 cup ranch dressing or your choice of dressing (optional)

Instructions:

1. **Cook the Chicken:**
    - Heat the olive oil in a skillet over medium heat.
    - Season the chicken breasts or thighs with salt and black pepper.
    - Add the chicken to the skillet and cook for 6-7 minutes per side, or until cooked through and no longer pink in the center.
    - Remove the chicken from the skillet and let it rest for a few minutes. Slice or shred the chicken into bite-sized pieces.
2. **Add BBQ Sauce:**
    - Return the sliced or shredded chicken to the skillet and pour in the BBQ sauce and honey (if using).
    - Stir to coat the chicken evenly and cook for an additional 2-3 minutes until heated through and the sauce has thickened slightly.
3. **Assemble the Wraps:**
    - Lay out the tortillas on a flat surface.
    - Spread a layer of ranch dressing or your preferred dressing (if using) on each tortilla.
    - Add a layer of shredded lettuce to the center of each tortilla.
    - Top with BBQ chicken, sliced red onion, bell peppers, shredded cheese, sliced jalapeños (if using), and avocado slices (if using).
    - Sprinkle with chopped fresh cilantro (if using).

4. **Wrap and Serve:**
   - Fold in the sides of each tortilla and then roll it up tightly from the bottom to the top.
   - Slice the wraps in half on a diagonal for easy serving.

Tips:

- **Make-Ahead:** BBQ chicken can be made ahead of time and stored in the refrigerator for up to 3 days. Reheat before assembling the wraps.
- **Vegetable Variations:** Feel free to add other vegetables like tomatoes, cucumbers, or shredded carrots.
- **Spicy Option:** Add hot sauce or more jalapeños if you like extra heat.
- **Grill Option:** For added flavor, you can grill the chicken and wrap ingredients. Simply preheat the grill and cook the chicken until done. You can also grill the wraps briefly for a crispy texture.

BBQ Chicken Wraps are a flavorful and customizable meal that's perfect for a quick dinner or a fun lunch. Enjoy these tasty wraps with your favorite sides or as is!

Cheese and Veggie Stuffed Mushrooms

Ingredients:

- **For the Stuffed Mushrooms:**
    - 12 large button or cremini mushrooms
    - 2 tablespoons olive oil, divided
    - 1 small onion, finely chopped
    - 2 cloves garlic, minced
    - 1 cup chopped fresh spinach or kale
    - 1/2 cup diced bell peppers (any color)
    - 1/2 cup shredded cheese (cheddar, mozzarella, or a mix)
    - 1/4 cup grated Parmesan cheese
    - 1/4 cup breadcrumbs (plain or seasoned)
    - 1 teaspoon dried oregano
    - 1/2 teaspoon dried thyme
    - Salt and black pepper, to taste
    - Fresh parsley, chopped (for garnish, optional)

Instructions:

1. **Prepare the Mushrooms:**
    - Preheat your oven to 375°F (190°C).
    - Clean the mushrooms with a damp paper towel. Carefully remove the stems and set them aside. You'll use the mushroom caps for stuffing.
2. **Prepare the Filling:**
    - Finely chop the mushroom stems.
    - Heat 1 tablespoon of olive oil in a skillet over medium heat.
    - Add the chopped mushroom stems, onion, and garlic. Cook for about 5 minutes, or until the vegetables are softened and the mushrooms have released their moisture.
    - Add the chopped spinach or kale and diced bell peppers to the skillet. Cook for an additional 2-3 minutes until the spinach or kale is wilted and the bell peppers are tender.
    - Remove from heat and stir in the shredded cheese, Parmesan cheese, and breadcrumbs. Mix until well combined. Season with dried oregano, dried thyme, salt, and black pepper.
3. **Stuff the Mushrooms:**
    - Brush the mushroom caps with the remaining 1 tablespoon of olive oil.
    - Place the mushroom caps on a baking sheet, gill side up.
    - Spoon the cheese and veggie mixture into each mushroom cap, packing it in gently.
4. **Bake:**

- Bake in the preheated oven for 15-20 minutes, or until the mushrooms are tender and the tops are golden brown.
5. **Garnish and Serve:**
    - Remove from the oven and let cool slightly.
    - Garnish with chopped fresh parsley if desired.
    - Serve warm.

Tips:

- **Cheese Options:** You can use different types of cheese based on your preference, such as goat cheese, feta, or a cheese blend.
- **Breadcrumbs:** For a gluten-free option, use gluten-free breadcrumbs or omit them entirely.
- **Vegetable Variations:** Feel free to experiment with other vegetables like zucchini, carrots, or mushrooms. Just make sure to finely chop them so they cook evenly.
- **Make-Ahead:** The stuffed mushrooms can be assembled ahead of time and stored in the refrigerator for up to 24 hours before baking.

These Cheese and Veggie Stuffed Mushrooms are a flavorful and elegant addition to any meal or party platter. Enjoy these savory bites!

Turkey Meatball Subs

Ingredients:

- **For the Turkey Meatballs:**
    - 1 pound (450 grams) ground turkey
    - 1/4 cup breadcrumbs (plain or Italian)
    - 1/4 cup grated Parmesan cheese
    - 1 large egg
    - 2 cloves garlic, minced
    - 1/4 cup finely chopped fresh parsley
    - 1 teaspoon dried oregano
    - 1/2 teaspoon dried basil
    - Salt and black pepper, to taste
- **For the Subs:**
    - 1 1/2 cups marinara sauce (store-bought or homemade)
    - 4 sub rolls or hoagie buns
    - 1 cup shredded mozzarella cheese
    - 1/4 cup grated Parmesan cheese (for topping)
    - Fresh basil or parsley, for garnish (optional)

Instructions:

1. **Prepare the Turkey Meatballs:**
    - Preheat your oven to 375°F (190°C).
    - In a large bowl, combine the ground turkey, breadcrumbs, grated Parmesan cheese, egg, minced garlic, chopped parsley, dried oregano, dried basil, salt, and black pepper.
    - Mix until all ingredients are well incorporated, but be careful not to overmix.
2. **Form and Bake the Meatballs:**
    - Shape the mixture into meatballs, about 1 to 1.5 inches in diameter. Place them on a baking sheet lined with parchment paper or lightly greased.
    - Bake in the preheated oven for 20-25 minutes, or until the meatballs are cooked through and have an internal temperature of 165°F (74°C).
3. **Prepare the Subs:**
    - While the meatballs are baking, heat the marinara sauce in a large saucepan over medium heat.
    - Once the meatballs are done, add them to the marinara sauce and let them simmer for about 5 minutes to soak up the flavors.
4. **Assemble the Subs:**
    - Cut the sub rolls or hoagie buns lengthwise, but not all the way through, so they remain connected on one side.
    - Spoon some marinara sauce onto each roll.

- Place 3-4 meatballs on each roll.
- Spoon more marinara sauce over the meatballs.
- Sprinkle shredded mozzarella cheese evenly over the meatballs and sauce.
- Optionally, sprinkle additional grated Parmesan cheese on top.
5. **Melt the Cheese:**
    - Place the assembled subs on a baking sheet and put them under the broiler for 2-3 minutes, or until the cheese is melted and bubbly. Watch carefully to avoid burning.
6. **Garnish and Serve:**
    - Remove from the oven and garnish with fresh basil or parsley, if desired.
    - Serve immediately while warm.

Tips:

- **Sauce Options:** You can use homemade marinara sauce or your favorite store-bought version. For extra flavor, add a pinch of red pepper flakes to the sauce if you like a bit of heat.
- **Cheese Variations:** Try different types of cheese, such as provolone or cheddar, for a different twist.
- **Make-Ahead:** The meatballs can be made ahead of time and stored in the refrigerator for up to 3 days or frozen for up to 3 months. Reheat in the sauce before assembling the subs.

Turkey Meatball Subs are a satisfying and flavorful option that offers a lighter take on a classic favorite. Enjoy these tasty sandwiches with a side of salad or baked fries!

Chicken Burrito Bowls

Ingredients:

- **For the Chicken:**
    - 1 pound (450 grams) boneless, skinless chicken breasts or thighs
    - 2 tablespoons olive oil
    - 1 tablespoon chili powder
    - 1 teaspoon ground cumin
    - 1 teaspoon smoked paprika
    - 1/2 teaspoon garlic powder
    - 1/2 teaspoon onion powder
    - 1/2 teaspoon dried oregano
    - Salt and black pepper, to taste
- **For the Rice (or Quinoa):**
    - 1 cup long-grain white rice or quinoa
    - 2 cups water or chicken broth
    - 1/2 teaspoon salt
- **For the Bowl Toppings:**
    - 1 cup black beans (canned or cooked), drained and rinsed
    - 1 cup corn kernels (fresh, frozen, or canned)
    - 1 cup cherry tomatoes, halved
    - 1 cup shredded lettuce or baby spinach
    - 1 avocado, sliced
    - 1/2 cup shredded cheese (cheddar, Monterey Jack, or your choice)
    - 1/4 cup chopped fresh cilantro
    - Lime wedges, for serving
- **For the Optional Dressing:**
    - 1/2 cup sour cream or Greek yogurt
    - 1 tablespoon lime juice
    - 1 teaspoon taco seasoning or hot sauce (to taste)

Instructions:

1. **Cook the Chicken:**
    - In a small bowl, combine the chili powder, cumin, smoked paprika, garlic powder, onion powder, dried oregano, salt, and black pepper.
    - Rub the spice mixture evenly over the chicken breasts or thighs.
    - Heat the olive oil in a large skillet over medium-high heat.
    - Add the chicken and cook for 6-7 minutes per side, or until cooked through and no longer pink in the center. The internal temperature should reach 165°F (74°C).
    - Remove the chicken from the skillet and let it rest for a few minutes before slicing or shredding.

2. **Prepare the Rice (or Quinoa):**
    - Rinse the rice or quinoa under cold water.
    - In a medium saucepan, bring the water or chicken broth to a boil.
    - Add the rice or quinoa and salt. Reduce the heat to low, cover, and simmer until tender and cooked through. This typically takes about 15 minutes for rice and 12-15 minutes for quinoa.
    - Remove from heat and let it sit, covered, for 5 minutes. Fluff with a fork.
3. **Prepare the Toppings:**
    - While the chicken and rice/quinoa are cooking, prepare the bowl toppings.
    - If using frozen corn, thaw it in the microwave or briefly cook in a skillet.
4. **Make the Optional Dressing:**
    - In a small bowl, mix together the sour cream or Greek yogurt, lime juice, and taco seasoning or hot sauce. Adjust to taste.
5. **Assemble the Burrito Bowls:**
    - In each bowl, start with a base of rice or quinoa.
    - Top with sliced or shredded chicken.
    - Add black beans, corn, cherry tomatoes, shredded lettuce or spinach, avocado slices, and shredded cheese.
    - Garnish with chopped fresh cilantro and a wedge of lime.
6. **Serve:**
    - Serve the Chicken Burrito Bowls with the optional dressing on the side, or drizzle it over the top.

Tips:

- **Customizable Toppings:** Feel free to add other toppings like diced bell peppers, pickled jalapeños, or sliced olives.
- **Meal Prep:** These bowls are great for meal prep. Assemble individual bowls and store them in the refrigerator for up to 4 days. Add fresh avocado and dressing just before serving.
- **Vegetarian Option:** Substitute the chicken with roasted vegetables, tofu, or another plant-based protein for a vegetarian version.

Chicken Burrito Bowls are a delicious and satisfying meal that's easy to customize to your preferences. Enjoy this flavorful dish any day of the week!

Pita Bread Pizzas

Ingredients:

- **For the Pita Bread Pizzas:**
    - 4 pita breads (whole wheat or white)
    - 1/2 cup pizza sauce (store-bought or homemade)
    - 1 1/2 cups shredded mozzarella cheese
    - 1/2 cup grated Parmesan cheese (optional)
    - 1/2 cup sliced pepperoni, cooked sausage, or your choice of protein
    - 1/2 cup sliced bell peppers (any color)
    - 1/2 cup sliced black olives
    - 1/2 cup sliced mushrooms
    - 1/4 cup chopped red onion
    - 1/4 cup sliced cherry tomatoes
    - 1 teaspoon dried oregano
    - 1 teaspoon dried basil
    - Salt and black pepper, to taste
    - Fresh basil or parsley, for garnish (optional)

Instructions:

1. **Preheat Oven:**
    - Preheat your oven to 400°F (200°C).
2. **Prepare the Pita Bread:**
    - Place the pita breads on a baking sheet or pizza stone. If using a baking sheet, you may want to line it with parchment paper for easy cleanup.
3. **Add the Sauce:**
    - Spread a thin layer of pizza sauce over each pita bread, leaving a small border around the edges.
4. **Add Cheese and Toppings:**
    - Sprinkle a generous amount of shredded mozzarella cheese over the sauce on each pita.
    - Add your choice of toppings: pepperoni, sausage, bell peppers, olives, mushrooms, red onion, cherry tomatoes, etc.
    - Sprinkle with grated Parmesan cheese, if using.
5. **Season:**
    - Sprinkle dried oregano, dried basil, salt, and black pepper over the top of the pizzas.
6. **Bake:**
    - Bake in the preheated oven for 10-12 minutes, or until the cheese is melted and bubbly and the edges of the pita are crisp.
7. **Garnish and Serve:**

- Remove the pita pizzas from the oven and let them cool for a few minutes.
- Garnish with fresh basil or parsley if desired.
- Slice into wedges and serve.

Tips:

- **Customizable:** You can customize these pita bread pizzas with any of your favorite toppings. Try adding cooked chicken, bacon, artichoke hearts, or even fresh herbs.
- **Vegetarian:** For a vegetarian option, load up on vegetables and use a meat-free cheese substitute if needed.
- **Quick and Easy:** These pizzas are perfect for a quick meal or snack. They're also great for kids to make their own pizzas with their choice of toppings.

Pita Bread Pizzas are a versatile and easy-to-make option that's sure to please everyone. Enjoy your personalized pizzas fresh out of the oven!